Feltmaking
and Wool Magic

JORIE JOHNSON

GLOUCESTER MASSACHUSETTS

QUARRY BOOKS

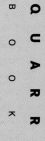

TO THE SHEEP OF THE WORLD

Sheep have been man's reliable friends for centuries. They are a gift from the heavens whose natural wool is strong, warm, beautiful, and of a miraculous nature.

I have lived in Japan for the last seventeen years, but I have introduced feltmaking to people around the world in Europe, Scandinavia, Central and Eastern Asia, and the United States. Traveling has given me many opportunities to research as well as evaluate teaching techniques, regardless of language handicaps.

The original version of this book was written in Japanese, and designed to introduce the story of wool fiber and contemporary feltmaking techniques to students of all ages. My own Japanese language skills were poor, and I was in need of a book to help teach the details of feltmaking. Since publication of the Japanese edition I have received many requests for the English version; please note that this book includes new and updated information, so it is not simply a translation.

I remember the first exhibition I had in Japan. Several guests asked me, "How did you weave this work? How did you color the surface?" I was surprised to hear these questions, as the answers seemed obvious, but my response hasn't changed much since then. "This work is not woven, knitted, or even stitched. This is a shrunken work called felt!" The explanation sounds better in Japanese but the fact that the question came up showed many people's unfamiliarity with the Silk Road textile technique, the color blending possibilities with wool, how to make cut shapes from prefelt, or how to use supplementary materials for adding character to the surface of felt.

Without the strong interest of my felt students of all ages, my friends and expedition companions, and a dedicated Joi Rae Textile staff, this text and the many photographs would not have appeared in any language. Special recognition goes to Atsuko Ikuno, Naomi Takagi, Eiko Akiyama, Hirotsugu Kubo, Shiro Matsui, Keiko Kawashima, Mary E. Burkett, the Office of the Shōsō-in, and I.W.S. Japan for helping with and supporting my ideas; and to Helen Umakoski and Nou-ka Yang for facilitating the English translation. Thank you to Rockport Publishers for taking this book on board and to their efficient staff for piloting it to dock.

A big thank you to my parents, especially my father, Thomas L. Johnson, a wool man in his own right, who introduced me to the world of textiles and who first lectured me on the wonders of the wool fiber.

—Jorie Johnson

Spring shearing,
North American Almanac,
June, 1828

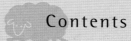

Contents

SECTION 1: GETTING STARTED

6   Living with Felt
10   Materials and Tools for Feltmaking
14   The Nine Conditions of Felting

SECTION 2: FELT PROJECTS

17   Simple Balls and Shapes
20   Pet Portraits
24   Prefelt Color Samples
26   Breed Samples
30   Crescent Pendants
33   Flower Bouquets
37   Doggie Toys
41   Mouse
45   Baby Bee Boots
49   Fun Shoulder Bags
56   Jack and Jill Dolls
61   A Lady's Hat
67   Little Lady's Flower Beret
73   Rainbow Jumper
79   Fabric for Short Vests
83   Washing Machine Samples
85   Elegant Long Vest
89   Flat Braided Muffler
94   Mohair Yarn Scarf
98   Warm Winter Slippers
103   Colorful Carpets

SECTION 3: TECHNIQUES AND HISTORY

109   Carding Wool
111   Washing Fleece
113   Popular Sheep Fleece
114   The Anatomy of Wool Fibers
118   Sheep Breed Samples
120   Traditional and Contemporary Motifs
122   The History of Felt
129   Healthy Postures in Feltmaking
131   Glossary
134   Where to Shop
135   Selected Bibliography
136   About the Author

FELT: A SECOND SKIN

Long ago, sheep appeared on earth as a special gift to humankind. From ancient times onwards, their amazing wooly fleece has been used to make felt, which in addition to animal hides was essential for shelter and protection from the harsh elements of nature. Felt has also been used in many shamanic and religious rituals, such as Tibetan wedding carpets, as well as for dolls intended to protect the well-being of a family, for shrouds of corpses, and for tapestries hung on the walls of the tombs of the wealthy. Recently, felt artifacts (hats and boot liners) were discovered in a tomb at the outskirts of the western desert in China. These objects date back to 1400 to 1200 B.C, but anthropologists have long believed that felt was being used well before the Bronze II Age (ca. 2600 B.C.).

Doll and bag found in a Barach shaman yurt, Inner Mongolia, 1930

Such exceptionally old felt artifacts are far and few between, and may have either been overlooked by art historians or simply did not have the lasting strength as compared to other plied and woven textiles of the same age.

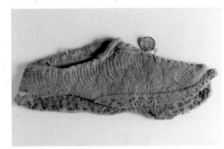

Quilted shoe, China

MODERN-DAY USE

Many people around the world still use felt in their daily lives. In Scandinavia, for example, a grandmother may make warm, thick winter boots and mittens for her grandchildren and husband. In the Andes Mountains of South America, people make felt hats to protect their heads from the cold in winter and the sun's rays in summer. In Central Asia, men

Boots and bag, Sweden

and women lay felt carpets on the dirt floors inside their yurt tents. They sit and sleep on them because the cold air cannot penetrate the dense carpet, and the insulating wool keeps the warm air inside. We can also see wonderful examples of sheltering capes that herders wear in the mountains to protect themselves from the wind, rain, snow, and sun.

Across Asia, families work together to make large felt panels that hang on wooden frames (called *pao* in Chinese and *ger* in Mongolian), forming the walls and roofs of their yurt tents. The yurt is a very practical shelter for these nomadic people who move to new grazing ground every few months: its round structure is very strong, making it hard for the wind to blow it over; its lattice-type walls can

Shirmak stitched carpet, Kazakh

collapse and expand; and its felt wall sections roll up easily. Because felt made from wool is a renewable material, it has provided protection from the elements for thousands of years. Elsewhere, the cowboys of North America and the bushwhackers of Australia wear hats made from sheep wool as well as a variety of felted animal fur, including antelope and rabbit.

Felt is also a practical material for everyday objects. It is used inside pianos and automobiles to produce certain sounds and isolate others. When felt is made from very fine fibers even the fragile surface of a thin cassette tape can be run across a tiny square of it!

Mongolian women making boots outside of their summer yurt, 1991

In Japan, wool is a relatively new material (sheep are not indigenous to Japan), compared to the traditional silk and bast, which are made from certain plant fibers. Although research and production of wool didn't begin in Japan until the late 1800s, the country produces felt for thin carpets called *mousen*, as well as for felt-tipped pens, tennis balls, and many industrial products. The Shōsō-in collection in Nara, Japan, has exquisite examples of felt carpets with floral designs, called *kasen*, which experts believe were imported as gifts and used by Emperor Shoumo more than 1,200 years ago. This very fine collection exemplifies the high level of achievement using this technique as early as the eighth century. Today, one finds felt almost everywhere, and, in general, the ancient handmade techniques and the modern machine processes are fundamentally the same.

Shepherd's Kepenek Cape, Turkey

World War II felt tabi socks, Japan

Shōsō-in flower medallion carpet, Japan

At the same time, pressure and friction help initiate the migration of the fibers. With continued action and pressure exerted over time, the individual fibers become entangled into a mass fabric referred to as felt. The more pressure and time exerted, the greater the percentage of entanglement, or shrinkage, occurs.

WHY SHEEP WOOL?

The anatomy of the wool fiber is very interesting. Because the fiber is hair that grows from the sheep's skin, it is also useful near human skin for its insulating and water-repelling properties. Thus, a sheep can be viewed as one of man's best friends. Wool fiber is unlike that of cotton, linen, silk, or polyester, because wool has minute scales, or cuticles, that are etched into the fiber surface as it grows and extends from follicles in the skin.

The fiber itself is a wavy spiral, making it flexible enough to be stretched but with the ability to spring back to its original curl length. Under controlled conditions of pH change, moisture, and heat, one can make the scales unfurl from the fiber shaft and act like hooks.

There are over 2,500 felt parts inside an upright piano.

MAN AND SHEEP

In ages past, in different areas around the world, whether colder climates or in higher altitudes, mountain goats and sheep were indigenous. Their mixed color fleece was gray, beige, brown, and dark brown to nearly black, the natural camouflage colors; some were speckled with bits of white. About 10,000 years ago, humans learned how to raise sheep and shear their fleece. They began to breed different types of sheep to produce fibers of consistent colors and lengths. In addition, they dyed wool in special colors and used it in different ways, such as felting, spinning, knitting, and weaving. The illustrations below show the simple, traditional process of feltmaking discovered long, long ago.

THE CHINESE FELT CARPET-MAKING TECHNIQUE

During the Edo Period in the year 1804, a shrine priest from Nagasaki recorded the process of basic felt carpet making as demonstrated by several Chinese artisans brought to Japan. In the illustrations below, five carpets are being made as a set. For such a project, it is important to make the overall size and thickness of each carpet the same, and to weigh the materials carefully before-hand (fig. 1, below).

Sometimes, if the percentage of lanolin (the natural grease in wool) is very high, the wool must be washed in order to release the oil. Wet wool must be dried thoroughly before its true weight can be determined. Only then can the wool be used in a calculation of the amount needed for a project. These days, it is easy to buy prewashed, dyed, and carded wool, and projects usually start with weighing the wool.

To produce a well-matted felt fabric, the staples of wool clipped from the sheep must be opened up (fig. 1, bottom). This process allows dirt and grass to drop or be picked out easily.

While making a simple toy ball requires only one's hands as tools, creating a wide, flat work, such as these carpets, calls for equipment—traditionally, a grass or reed mat was used. Today, thick plastic sheeting or a length of heavy insulating bubble wrap is a suitable substitute. The wool is carefully and evenly spread out over the mat and then dampened thoroughly with water (fig. 2).

It is preferable now to use a plastic bottle filled with felting solution made with water and soap. (See page 13 for more information on felting solution.) When the mat is rolled and tied securely, the layers of arranged wool are safely preserved. To initiate the felting process, the bundle is rolled or kicked back and forth for ten to fifteen minute sessions (fig. 3). Bundles for smaller objects can be rolled back and forth on a kitchen table using your hands and arms. This part of the process is fun and easy, but also very mysterious. Why does this work?

The simple action of rolling the bundle back and forth activates the migration of the fibers as they rub against each other. The secret of why wool is the best fiber for felting is that each protein fiber has a scaly surface. The scales, which are invisible to the naked eye, grow out of the skin and are etched into the surface of the fiber. Three actions—the added moisture relaxing the fibers, the rolling motion creating friction, and the consistent agitation lasting over a period of time—produce a felted fabric that is quite miraculous. Though this process is called shrinking, the wool fiber itself doesn't shrink. Instead, it is the result of the mass of fibers, rubbing and curling around each other, entangling themselves, more closely and tightly together. When the space between the fibers disappears, the result is a strong, tough fabric that may have shrunk to 40 to 50 percent of its original size.

MAKING FELT CARPETS AT MIZUJINJA SHRINE, NAGASAKI, JAPAN

Fig. 1 Weighing and separating the wool

Fig. 2 Spreading out and wetting the wool

Fig. 3 Rolling the secured bundle

Fig. 4 Checking the quality

The wool is not suitable for felting if the fibers have difficulty slipping past each other to start the process. In this case, it doesn't matter how many hours are spent in the felting process, the fibers will never become a tight, stiff fabric. For this reason its important to chose the proper wool for felting.

During the rolling process, it is best to frequently open the bundle and check the progress of the matting fibers, especially in the beginning. This is the time when there is more space between the fibers, and more movement will occur within the design layers. Also, one can check the quality of the work, remove any undesirable matter, such as grass (lunch for a sheep), and add extra fibers in any thin areas (fig. 4). When the layers of wool have turned into a soft fabric, the shrinking process will be faster without the mat. Begin by rolling the wool on a tabletop; after it tightens up, try stamping on it in a tub of hot water to achieve even greater shrinkage (fig. 5).

Water temperature and the degree of acidity/alkalinity (pH) in the solution will affect the condition of the fibers. In particular, applying hot water and soap changes the time necessary for felting. Adding shampoo or soap to very hot water (107°F [42°C] or higher) helps to moisten and relax the wool, so the individual fibers then can slip pass and entangle with each other. The higher pH of the soap solution also causes the fiber's outer surface to open more readily, thus creating more surface area and causing the hooklike scales to clasp together. Industrial felting methods, on the other hand, often employ acid solutions for the same purpose.

Once the work is well shrunk and has a suitable shape and firmness, it is important to wash out the soap residue (fig. 6). If it is a smaller-sized work, rinse it, and then do one of three things: Put it in a salad or clothes spinner for several seconds to a minute, roll it in a towel, or hang it outside to drip dry.

One can make felt from natural-color or dyed fleece, or choose to work in white wool and dye the felt after completion (fig. 7). During the dyeing process, the fibers will have a tendency to continue shrinking, which can either be a good thing or a bad thing, depending on the project. Because dyeing conditions promote shrinking, some muscle power can be saved in the rolling stages. For example, one can dye some almost-finished felt boots in a nearly boiling dye bath, and then continue rolling them to achieve the desired size. To finish the work properly, it must be steam-ironed or rolled with a heavy rod, stretched, shaped into its final form, and then left to air dry completely (fig. 8).

This overview of the simple, ancient process of feltmaking shows why felt has long been man's second skin. Very little equipment is needed to get started; all of it can easily be found around the house or at local do-it-yourself and craft stores. Also, there is no need to dye a project, unless it is desired; natural sheep wool makes a strong, durable felt fabric. And since sheep fleece can be shorn once or twice a year, the supply of wool is never ending. Feltmaking is very eco-friendly and can help teach students of all ages about the natural processes and uses of animals. Some domestic pet furs and hairs can also be felted, such as an English sheepdog's undercoat. A blend of 15 percent long rabbit or cat fur and 85 percent good felting wool, such as merino, can work as well.

Luckily, crafters don't have to raise their own sheep for a reliable wool supply! It is not difficult to get good wool for felting. To get started, check the list of suppliers or search the Internet (see Where to Shop, page 134). Although people today no longer have to rely solely on wool and feltmaking for warmth and shelter, the magic and fun of making things for family and friends remains strong. Anyone of nearly any age will enjoy learning this ancient craft and creating wonderful, one-of-a-kind treasures.

Fig. 5 Treading the felt carpet

Fig. 6 Washing the carpet

Fig. 7 Dyeing the felt carpet

Fig. 8 Stretching and shaping the felt carpets

Various tools and materials play an important role in feltmaking. You can often find recyclable materials and simple tools around the house or buy inexpensive items to get started. In addition, leftover yarn from knitting and weaving projects can be used for decorative motifs.

BASE WOOL FIBER

Base wool constitutes the underlying structure and reinforces the work. The fibers from the finer sheep breeds easily intertwine with each other and will also laminate well with an auxiliary design motif material, such as silk organza or lace fabric. Base wool includes the so-called merino tops (60s to 64s and finer, where *s* is the unit of fiber quality count), which is an appropriate wool fineness for quick, small felting projects such as jewelry and toys, as well as for larger items worn close to the body, such as soft berets and shawls. Wool readied in the "tops" form, sometimes referred to as sliver, is washed, dyed, or natural-color raw wool that has been combed and prepared in a continuous ropelike form. During combing, the fibers are aligned in the same direction, making it is easy to draw out thin layers of uniform thickness during the early stages of the work. By dividing the ropelike top, it becomes a convenient material for making felt strings and bag straps or strands for braided scarves.

A crossbreed wool, with a general coarseness of 56s to 58s, is a good material for bags, brimmed hats, vests, and small mats. Flat braiding longer fibers, such as romney or corriedale, are suitable for spongy scarves and blankets. (See page 113 for a wool fineness chart.) Be sure to test several types and don't limit yourself to a narrow selection.

RAW WOOL

Wool, mainly from sheep, is used to produce felt fabrics, as well as yarns for knitwear and woven textiles. Usually quite greasy in its original state, raw wool is usually washed, or scoured, and sent through several processes to prepare it for convenient use. It is available in a variety of prepared stages, such as fleece, washed or scoured, sliver or tops, web, batt, and needled (for more on these terms, see the Glossary on page 131).

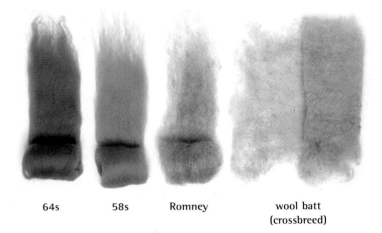

| 64s | 58s | Romney | wool batt (crossbreed) |

BATT FORM

Washed wool that has been through a carding machine, which combs and aligns the fibers in the same direction, and formed into a wide sheet with even thickness, is called a batt. A drum carder, which is a two-cylinder machine, has drums with thousands of sharp wire hooks, or teeth, attached to the surface. As the drums rotate in opposite directions, the fibers are pulled apart, aligned, and combed into a batt. This is the most convenient form of all processed wool for making larger projects such as fabrics or carpets. Batts are easy for children to handle (the fibers in the top form are slippery). Drum carders are available in smaller sizes and are useful for the home crafter, as well as in sizes suitable for industry.

For smaller amounts of wool, paddlelike hand carders, similar to but larger than pet brushes, are sold in pairs and are available through craft suppliers. Worked between both hands, these carders are ideal for small amounts of color blending; this technique produces nuances of shades and is an alternative to dyeing the wool a solid color at the start. Moreover, wool and other animal hair, such as mink, dog, or exotic pet, used as base or motif material, can be blended together in correct proportions using carding tools.

Materials for decorative motifs

MATERIALS FOR DECORATION AND STRENGTH

The supplementary materials listed below (and shown above) are items which, when combined with wool during the felting process, create variations in textured surfaces and motif expressions.

A. Novelty yarns and ornamental thread Wool, blended specialty yarns of 70 to 100 percent wool content, mohair, some metallic threads, as well as the multitude of new product blends, can be laid on top, or just under, the surface of a thin layer of wool. During the felting process it is interesting to watch how the motif changes character as it embeds in the felt fabric. Contour lines, thin stripes, and small designs are easy to make with yarn. Try writing names and dates or adding fringes. In addition, single non-plied yarn, sometimes referred to as pencil roving, can be hand drawn and slightly twisted from color tops and added to the decorative layer. Handspun pencil roving is traditionally used by nomads in Central Asia.

B. Decorative silk and polyester netting fabrics Sheer, gauzy silk and synthetic netting may be felted into the surface of the base wool layer. Laminate coarser fabrics together by seaming them with wool or sandwiching a layer of wool between them to create unique crinkled surface textures. Cut-fabric edges can be easily encased in wool and then felted into a smooth finished felt band, thus eliminating the need to hand stitch rolled edges.

C. Viscose scarf Used in the same manner as silk organza or georgette, this airy viscose fabric can be laminated to a wool base to produce thin felt fabrics with a supple drape.

D. Cotton cheesecloth Cheesecloth is useful as an inner reinforcement layer, when you need a thin, pliable, yet strong felt fabric. Laminating fine wool layers to either or both sides of the cloth hides the cheesecloth. If areas of the gauzy cloth are left uncovered, the contrast between the felted wool and the cloth layer adds a unique character to the work.

E. Dyed silk floss Laying silk top or floss on the surface of the wool produces a brushlike, lusterous line on the piece. The resulting contrast between the matte finish of the wool and lustrous silk is quite interesting.

F. Multicolor wool batt (merino) Similar to mixing or marbling oil colors, using a hand carder creates color nuances. Blending in black or white wool deepens or lightens colors, or you can achieve multicolor rainbow gradations. Color blending finer, rather than coarser, wool produces subtler effects. As a rule, it is faster to use hand carders to make a desired color blend than to dye white wool.

G. Prefelt and woven fabrics Lightweight, minimally felted fabrics called prefelts (see color sample on page 24), as well as some woven or knitted woolen (non-boiled) fabrics, can be used as additional motifs that adhere to the surface during the felting process. Cutting simple forms, such as flowers, leaves, letters, and geometric shapes, from these softer and more open fabrics simplifies and speeds production of multiple motifs. In areas with intricate designs, it is easier and more consistent to cut them from prefelts rather than to try to control individual fibers.

Materials and Tools for Feltmaking

Many of the tools shown here are necessary for the projects in this book. Be sure to assemble this collection of items before starting your work.

1. Scale Weighing the wool helps determine the precise amount of wool required for each project. A pair of slippers, for instance, requires making two exact versions of the same shoe. Weighing the total amount of dry wool, and often individual layers, is a key step to ensuring success before starting a project. A good postal or kitchen scale, which registers small amounts (up to 16 oz. [350 g]) is handy. A digital or balance scale is necessary for small amounts of dye; scales that read up to 30 lbs. (13.6 kg) can weigh larger batts.

2. Hat and boot forms Forms are essential in making a particular size hat or pair of shoes, and, fortunately, there are several options to use in lieu of the traditional wooden hat form and shoe last (form). If you don't have a form on hand, sturdy household materials or objects such as a ball, handleless pan, bowl, or old shoe can work, or try carving a unique form from a dense Styrofoam block. Covering the surface of any hat form with a nylon stocking helps prevent the felt from slipping during final shaping. Conversely, covering a shoe form with a slippery plastic bag helps it slide into the ankle opening of the shoes.

3. Plastic bottle for felting solution Choose a plastic bottle that can withstand very hot water temperatures and then punch small holes in its cap. This tool controls the application of felting solution and ensures that it is dispersed evenly over the wool (see page 13, #18, for more on felting solution). An old aluminum saucepan with nail holes in the bottom makes a handy container for wetting larger projects such as carpets.

4. Washboard When substantial hardening is required in a difficult area, such as the ankle or heel of a pair of boots or slippers, rubbing the area against a washboard is effective. When selecting a washboard to use, check the width and depth of its rungs or depressions; spaces that are either too deep or too wide will not work. You can also use a glass washboard, a reed mat, a stainless-steel countertop with ribbed surface, or a tiled surface. (Washboards are more popular in Scandinavia because traditionally they use coarser wool, which can withstand rougher treatment.) NOTE: For the finer filaments of merino wool, a washboard surface is often too rough; bubble wrap (see page 13, #19) is a gentler alternative.

5. Towels There can never be enough towels in a felting studio. They are useful for absorbing excess felting solution, wiping sweat from a brow, or securely binding a project during the rolling process. Have several sizes on hand.

Materials and tools for feltmaking

6. Steam iron and steamer A cold felt fabric is harder to shape than a warm one. Applying steam allows the entangled fibers to relax; the felt can then be shaped to a form or be pulled out to straighten its edges. To reheat the fibers between rolling sessions when making larger fabrics, it is faster to fold the piece in thirds, roll it up, and place it inside a large steamer for several minutes, rather than to constantly apply more hot felting solution. A steam iron is used when working with an electric sander to keep water at a safe minimum (see page 92 for more on the safe use of electric sanders).

7. Hand carders This tool comes as a pair of paddles, each with a set of sharp, metal wire teeth sticking out from one side. Carders are used to comb the tangled fibers into a single direction, forming small square batts. In addition, carders are handy for color blending as well as for mixing different fibers and furs. There are a variety of models on the market, so look for those with good balance and a comfortable feel.

8. Plastic net, polyester mesh, and lace-curtain fabric A net is used to cover dry wool before wetting, and is helpful in stabilizing the work and in flattening the wool layers during wetting without disturbing the design. A net is also helpful in stabilizing the wool surface when excess soapsuds need to be removed (a situation common to novices who have applied too much felting solution with a high soap concentration). The net holds the wool in place as dry towels press out and remove the "whipped cream" suds. Stiff, pressed screening is good for wide, flat areas because it does not stretch. Supple mesh or lace-curtain fabric is helpful for wetting the surface of a three-dimensional sculpture or toy.

9. Synthetic voile A cloth made from nylon, polyester, or other synthetic fiber is used when hardening felt in a washing machine. The wool is sandwiched between two layers of voile, which are then sewn together with basting stitches to prevent the wool from shifting during the initial machine-agitation hardening process.

10. Cotton cloth   This material is used as an outer wrapping layer, similar to a towel, to tightly secure the bundle and prevent the work from unwinding during the rolling process. The cotton wrapping prevents slipping on the worktable surface and at the same time absorbs excess moisture. A 40" x 40" (1 x 1m) cotton or linen tablecloth or old sheet is quite handy; larger projects require bigger pieces of fabric. Pure (100 percent) cotton, or linen, is preferable to polyester as it is more absorbent. Note that wool fibers can get caught in the loops of a terrycloth towel.

11. Pliers, permanent marker, and scissors   Pliers are helpful for reshaping and straightening the edges of a project; using only one's fingers will result in hand fatigue. A permanent marker is a good tool for drawing indelible outlines and designs on cardboard and plastic sheets. Sharp-edged scissors make cutting felt cloth easy and accurate.

12. Cardboard   Humidity-resistant plain cardboard with a maximum thickness of ⅛" (3 mm) is preferred. This cardboard is used as a resist pattern, keeping the layers of three-dimensional pieces such as bags, berets, and hats from adhering to each other. After cutting out the cardboard shape, prepare the pattern edges by binding them with clear tape. NOTE: If the same pattern is to be used repeatedly, substitute thin neoprene, thick vinyl table covering, or two pieces of bubble wrap, stitching the bubble sides together. For the bubble wrap, sew just inside the pattern line and then trim following the line.

13. Vinyl sheets   Medium-size garbage bags, thick plastic shopping bags, and plastic sheets are used to flip the work over between design stages. Thinner sheets, such as dry-cleaner bags without print on them and house painter's plastic drop cloths, are used to create a vacuum on the surface of the wool; this coaxes the fibers to start slipping and entangling amongst themselves. It may also be necessary to use plastic to protect the fragile outer layer of design elements, such as silk fabrics, from the rougher mat surface during the rolling process.

14. Plastic bags   During the agitation process woolen fibers tend to cling to bare, wet hands, making it difficult to slide your hands over the surface while working the wool. By covering your hands with small, smooth plastic bags, the surface fibers can be maneuvered more easily, and less soap is required for lubrication. Compare plastic bags, as some tend to grab the surface while others slide easily.

15. Bar soap   Unscented, additive-free soap, such as traditional olive oil soap, is helpful when you only need a minimal amount of suds. Simply rub the bar between your wet hands to create suds or, if the fabric or object is felted enough, apply the soap bar directly to the surface.

16. Plastic wrap   Resist-felting techniques use plastic wrap to cover areas that will not be attached to the main wool base. For example, loops and decorative "tails" extending from a work are wrapped in plastic wrap to keep them dry and unattached while their "roots" are being felted into the main body.

17. Rolling rods: stainless, plastic, foam, and wooden   These tools are the sturdy cores for the rolling stage. Hats and bags require rods from ½" to 1¼" (1.3 to 3 cm) in diameter and 16" to 24" (40 to 60 cm) long; larger projects call for thicker and longer pipes. In general, at the start of the rolling process, when the felt cloth is still soft and malleable, use thicker rods to avoid wrinkling. Then, once the felt cloth is more stable, substitute a narrower diameter rod for fulling, or hardening, the cloth more substantially. A heavier rod is also used during steam ironing, to help press the finished cloth by rolling it over the surface. A core rod of rolled bubble wrap, or foam "noodle," is useful when the design surface is bumpy or irregular, or you wish to create a wrinkled effect from the start. Also, when working with children, use this inexpensive tool to speed up the rolling process.

18. Shampoo/felting solution recipe   The shampoo, or soap-and-water solution, is called felting solution. Dissolving a small shot (1 teaspoon [5 ml]) of unscented, colorless, and conditioner-free shampoo, or grated bar or liquid soap, in 3 cups [710 ml] of hot water alters the pH of the water to a base, or alkaline, solution; this contributes to the change in the condition of the outer surface of the wool fiber and is safest during hand felting.

19. Bamboo mat, straw mat, and bubble wrap   Mats are used when a flat project is larger than the width of one's hand. Sushi mats or bamboo placemats are useful for making samples, color prefelts (see page 24), cords, and straps. Larger bamboo blinds are convenient for lengths of fabric and tapestries. Split bamboo blinds are recommended here because they are stronger and more flexible than reed blinds. Remember to wet the blind before starting so that the blind material will become more supple and last longer. For much larger and heavier works such as carpets, double-woven straw mats are best (two sheets of mats can be stitched together to achieve the proper width). These days, good quality double- or triple-woven, dense plastic mats may be substituted for bamboo or reed. Bubble wrap sheets have cushions of air, and thus, while rolling, one can apply a bouncier, three-dimensional pressure to the work. Bubble wrap allows finer work to acquire more volume as it is rolled up inside the sheet, and provides more leverage during rolling.

It is essential to keep these conditions in mind throughout the feltmaking process, as common mistakes will often hinder the process, and slow your progress.

1   **Wool quality**   The felting property of wool is due to its unique fiber characteristic, which, under special conditions, enables entanglement and causes mass shrinkage. The wool selected for a project should have similar traits to that of the desired finished product. For example, choose a finer filament wool for berets, a breed of medium coarseness for bags, and coarser wools for carpets. Using the right wool for a project will also help emphasize the expression of the work. Before using a wool, determine its best use: Is it better for spinning into yarn or does it felt up beautifully? (See the chart on page 132 explaining fiber categories.)

2   **Moisture: cold water, hot water, and steam**   Moisture in feltmaking is essential, as dry fibers do not felt. Wetting the fibers relaxes them, making them more flexible. Some industrial processes employ the absolute minimum of moisture by merely steaming the fibers to loosen them. Depending on the fineness and felting speed of the selected fiber, and the sheerness of the project, such as an evening stole, it may be suitable to start wetting with a minimum of cold felting solution rather than shocking the work with gallons of hot soapy water. On the other hand, coarser, slightly greasy wool, such as that recommended for durable carpets, might need repeated wetting with hot felting solution from the beginning.

3   **Heat**   Research shows that the hardening speed of felting is closely linked to temperature and humidity. To expedite the shrinking process, maintain a constant temperature of approximately 113°F (45°C). Don't forget that the temperature in the room, especially if it is chilly, may also have an effect on the speed of felting. Occasionally, you will come across wool that hardens very quickly. In such a case, when you start the project, take control of the hardening speed by using cold or warm water instead of hot felting solution, raising the temperature of felting solution as the work comes together and stabilizes. Fast hardening can cause irregularities, such as holes, in a finer-quality item. NOTE: Remember that the dyeing process may induce further hardening and shrinking in a completed work.

4   **pH Factor (The Hydrogen Ion Index)**   The pH value of the felting solution used will change the condition of the wool fiber, thus assisting in the felting process.

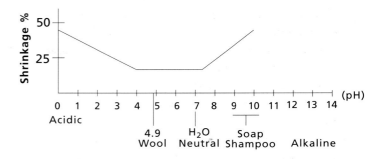

The condition of the wool fiber changes drastically when the pH balance is either less than 4 and between 7 and 10. In these solutions the rate of outer cuticle surface expansion will increase. Too high a pH (greater than 10), however, will irreparably damage the outer surface of the wool fiber. For hand felting it is recommended to use soap or shampoo with pH values of 7 to 10. Industry employs acid baths and steam because they use mechanical equipment, rather than human hands, to make felt. You should also be careful when using various vegetable dye solutions coupled with strong concentrations of the mordant, or color-fixing agent, not to damage the wool.

5 Soap and shampoo These additives help alter the pH factor to promote faster entangling of the fibers. In addition, soapsuds act as a lubricating agent to help the fibers slide more easily past each other (and, at times, clean the wool in the process). Select a soap or shampoo that is gentle to the skin, but without added conditioners, color, or scent. Small amounts of soapsuds, just enough to coat the fibers, will make the process go faster. Too much or too little (whipped-cream suds or dry-looking fibers) is not advantageous. The appropriate amount is important, but difficult to instruct, because water differs in hardness or softness, and because concentrations of soap products vary. Look for a light layer of fine suds on the surface as you rub your hands back and forth. **CAUTION:** When using strong acidic (as in industrial applications) or alkaline baths to promote faster shrinking, the use of rubber gloves is mandatory.

6 Vibration and agitation Various methods of agitation and vibration, such as rubbing, massaging, rolling, kneading, pounding, throwing, stomping, electric-sander motion, or machine washing are used to encourage wool fibers to migrate, enmesh, and form a fabric. It is imperative to learn which action is most appropriate at the various stages of the process. Using light pressure during the initial forming stage is best. Then, once it is obvious that the fibers have started to stabilize and form a fabric, add more pressure to the speed of rolling. Being too rough too soon may distort the pattern or cause irregular thickness or undesirable wrinkles in the fabric.

7 Pressure Once the clean fibers are wetted with felting solution, just the weight of your hands will create enough pressure to start the felting process. As the mass of fiber transforms into a ball or piece of cloth, applying more pressure and friction will encourage the ball or cloth to tighten further and harden faster. (For prefelt, felting, and hardening terms, see pages 131–133.)

8 Time factor Time is necessary to moisten, stimulate, shrink, and harden the wool; at each stage, the expression of the felt object will change. Using a timer to monitor rolling periods will help you determine when to stop felting in similar projects later on. To create high quality work with good design, it is important to accumulate experiential, quantitative data in the technique. In other words, time devoted to practice!

9 Project initiative and excitement People want to study feltmaking for various reasons: to make a warm, custom-made hat for winter, to benefit from its therapeutic qualities, or to teach children the fundamentals of the amazing sheep animal. Whatever the reason for making felt, if even only for the fun of it, the interest will lessen with fatigue. Therefore, it is important to take short breaks or consider finishing the item the following day in order to stay refreshed and clearheaded about the project and avoid tiring your muscles or overworking the wool itself.

THE WHYS AND HOW-TOs OF PREPARING FELTING SOLUTION (FS)

When using processed dyed wool, a soapy solution is essential for hand felting. The alkaline property of the soap encourages the fiber's surface, which is composed of a myriad of microscopic overlapping cuticles, to expand outward. When agitation is applied to the wetted fibers, these cuticles act like hooks and grab on to each other. Continued agitation causes the fibers to further entangle, resulting in a shrunken, or felted, fabric. Using fibers with a poor or nonexistent cuticle count, such as certain pet hairs, nylon, or cotton, will not work.

Factories use strong acid and alkaline chemicals for processing, but it is important for the hand felter to use soap that is gentle to skin, such as an unconditioned shampoo or natural olive oil soap. The amount of soap and hot water needed will vary according to the softness or hardness of the water supply in your area. With soft water, soap foams well and dissolves and washes out easily. When using hard water, soap lathers poorly and rinses out with difficulty. The pH factor in shampoo is just right for human skin. Do not use dishwashing or laundry detergent, as these products are concentrated and will irritate the skin with prolonged use.

Recipe for Felting Solution (FS)
Start by adding 1 teaspoon (5 ml) of finely grated olive soap or inexpensive, conditioner-free shampoo to 3 cups (710 ml) of hot water. (If you can find colorless and unscented shampoo, all the better. In fact, this may be a product you wouldn't want to use on your own hair.) Apply a small amount of felting solution evenly over the project and check the amount of suds created when the piece is lightly massaged. If the solution looks like whipped cream topping, adjust the proportions of water to soap. Too much foam will deter the fibers from felting. NOTE: There should never be more than a thin layer of fine suds on the surface of the work.

SIMPLE Balls
and Shapes

START FELTING BY LEARNING to turn bright fluffy wool into colorful balls. One interesting possibility is to make decorative pins out of felted balls with multicolored cores. These pins are felt balls cut in half to reveal striking inner spiral designs, similar to geode rocks, which reveal beautiful designs when split open. And with some experience, you can also turn these balls into exotic beads and buttons, unique flower pins, a variety of accessories, and even charming puppet heads.

MATERIALS

- White merino top for core, about .25 oz. (5 to 7g)*
- Dyed top wool for colored outer layer, about .25 oz. (5 to 7g)*
- Dyed wool for extra decoration, small amount in various colors
- Yarn, small amount
- Felting solution

> * Use either a digital scale or a balance scale using weights. Alternatively, stretch your fingers wide and measure a length (about 7" [18 cm]) from the pinkie finger to the thumb and use this to approximate the weight.

1

2

3

4

5

1 |

For the wool layers: Divide the white top into four sections widthwise; prepare three fluffy cloudlike piles by pulling out tufts of fibers and piling them on top of each other, leaving the fourth section as is to become the core. Make three piles of the dyed wool for the outer color in the same manner.

2 |

Take the fourth section of white top and roll it tightly into a ball. Wet it with felting solution. As tightly as possible, continue rolling up the core ball, adding each of the three white fluffy piles consecutively around the original core. Rotate the ball 90 degrees for each added layer. It is easier to roll each consecutive layer while working on a tabletop rather than in your hands in the air.

3 |

If the dry, spongy fibers become hard to handle, sprinkle felting solution over them to maintain better control. (When winter arrives, doesn't the cold air tend to stiffen up your body? But, as soon as you get into a hot bath, what happens? Your body starts to relax. Wool relaxes in the same way.)

4 |

Without using excess pressure or rubbing between layers (aside from wetting and smoothing the surface), add the dyed outer layers, continuing to tightly wrap the remaining three fluffy piles, rotating the ball 90 degrees for each added layer, and covering the white core completely. Wet with felting solution.

5 |

For the decorative design layer: Accent the surface of the wet ball by tightly wrapping a thin band of another color wool in different directions around the ball. Smooth the wrinkles with soapy hands.

Colorful ball buttons decorate a baby's coat.

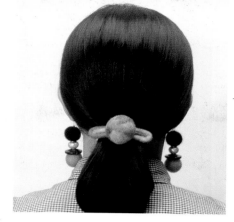

Silver bead, button, and felt-ball earrings complement the hairclip.

6 |

Further embellish the ball with novelty yarn wrapped snugly around the surface. Tuck the end under a cross point (where the yarn crosses over itself) to hold it in place. Wet the ball thoroughly.

7 |

With a bar of soap, lubricate the palms of your hands, and gently rotate and massage the ball between your hands. It is most important at the start to use simple, light pressure and a fair amount of soap to help round the ball.

8 |

The outer layer of fibers will naturally start to shrink and tighten first. After rolling the ball between your palms for a few minutes, do a pinch-test (see page 133) to check that the surface is tough enough to apply more pressure.

9 |

Once the ball has begun to harden, apply more direct pressure toward the center. Roll it around on a damp towel, as if you were making baker's rolls, with the direct weight of your arm and shoulder as added pressure. The towel will draw moisture from the ball, so when it begins to feel dry, sprinkle it with very hot felting solution. When the ball has shrunk to 25 to 30 percent of its original size, pinch-test it to see if the ball is as hard as desired; if not, keep rolling it. Try throwing it against the floor to see if it is hard enough to bounce back. When done, wash well, wring out moisture, and set aside to let dry completely.

6

7

8

9

ABC'S OF FELTMAKING

The important factors in shrinking wool are humidity and temperature (humidity + temperature = hot water) and soap (change in pH.) Adding friction and increasing pressure gradually over time will cause the wool fibers to migrate into a compact ball of wool.

CHILDREN CAN USE DYED WOOL TO "DRAW" the face of their favorite pet or friend in the same way they use crayons. They will have the satisfaction of completing these projects by themselves. For children whose attention span is limited, this project can be completed in three days by working just a couple of hours each day. An eight-year-old, with guidance from an adult, can easily tackle such a project. To display the wool "painting," make a complementary cardboard frame for the portrait before hanging.

Pet Portraits

MATERIALS

- Soft oil crayon or pastels
- White paper for drawing
- White wool for the base, preferably in easy-to-handle batts, .5 oz. (15 g)
- Variety of colored wool for drawing
- Yarn for outlines, minimal amount
- String or pipe cleaner, to hang portrait
- 1/8" (3 mm) cardboard, for frame

1 |

Draw an 8" (20.5 cm) square on a piece of paper. Have the children draw their favorite person or pet with soft oil crayons inside this frame. Take a 16" x 32" (40 x 80 cm) piece of bubble wrap and fold it in half with the smooth side up. With a permanent marker draw an 8" (20.5 cm) square in the center of one half of the smooth side of the bubble wrap.

2 |

Select bits of colorful wool to match the design areas in your drawing.

3 |

For the decorative design layer:
Open the bubble wrap and slip the original drawing underneath, centering it inside the drawn square. Taking small tufts of colored wool, dip them first in a bowl filled with felting solution, and then lay them directly onto the bubble wrap according to the drawing. For a face, start by laying out a piece of yarn to make the outline of the face and features (here, it is a bird's head and beak); then work on detailed parts such as the eyes and eyebrows. Lay enough colored wool to cover the entire drawing, working from the smallest details to the largest areas of color.

4 |

Use the ends of a pair of scissors or a fork to help arrange the smaller details.

5 |

For the base layer: After filling in the color design, which need not be a very thick layer, lay four alternating layers of white base wool (totaling 1/2 oz. [15 g]) at 90 degree angles to each other directly over the motif. They should extend to, but not exceed, the outlines of the square. This forms the base of the portrait.

6a |

Lay a plastic net over the base wool and sprinkle it generously with hot felting solution.

3

4

1

5

2

6a

6b

6b

With a slippery plastic bag over the child's hand, gently rub the net so that the felting solution spreads throughout the wool, pressing out any air at the same time.

6c

Fold the slightly extended edges back over along the black lines, toward the center, so the wool area remains an 8" x 8" (20.5 x 20.5 cm) square. Apply more felting solution to help the edges stay in place. Lightly massage the entire perimeter.

7

Fold over the bubble wrap, pressing tightly, and starting from the folded edge, roll it up around a ¾" (2 cm) –diameter rod. Secure both ends of the roll tightly with rubber bands, and wrap it in a damp towel.

8

Rolling: Using the entire length of your arm, move back and forth from your fingertips to elbows (one full count). While lightly pressing the upper body into the work, roll up and back for fifty counts. Open the bundle and turn the portrait 90 degrees; roll it up again, securing the ends with rubber bands. Roll fifty counts, then repeat this procedure for all four sides of the square.

9

With a small, slippery plastic bag over the child's hand, gently rub the design surface of the work with felting solution and extra soap, if necessary. To maintain a sharp square shape, pull out any dimples along the edges with your fingers.

10

If the design is well embedded after four sets of rolling, you may remove the bubble wrap, and with the right side up, roll the portrait directly onto the rod. If areas of the portrait have not joined with the white base then continue using the bubble wrap for the next four sets of rolling with the design side facing up.

6c

8

7

9

Giraffe

Parakeet

Chanting Monk

Wrap it securely in a towel and roll fifty counts. Repeat for all four sides, then turn it over, and roll the back side for fifty counts in four directions. Counting out loud makes this much more fun!

11

Rinse the portrait well in warm water; knead it like bread dough, making sure all the soap comes out. Stop when the length and width have shrunk by 1¼" (3 cm). To remove the excess water, roll it up in a towel or spin in clothes dryer or salad spinner for about thirty seconds. For a nicer finished look, press the portrait with a steam iron, correcting the shape, and leave it to dry thoroughly.

12a

For the frame: Use a craft knife or scissors to cut two pieces of cardboard, each ⅛" (3 mm) -thick, in an appropriate size frame for this portrait. Cut out a square in the center of one piece of cardboard to match the size of the felt portrait. Using a soft crayon, draw a design on the frame that complements the portrait.

12b

Attach the portrait to the frame using spongy double-sided tape. Glue the backing cardboard to the framed portrait. Alternatively, stitch the upper corners of the portrait through to the back of the frame using a large needle and thread and tie it to the frame.

13

To finish the frame, glue or tape a string or pipe-cleaner to the top or back of the frame and hang the portrait on the wall. Alternatively, tape a long, narrow triangle to the back of the frame for displaying the frame on a dresser or table. Ask the child these questions: Are you surprised that the drawing and the finished portrait are facing in opposite directions? Why would this happen?

10

11

12a

12b

13

Decorative inlaid prefelt sample

MATERIALS

- 3 colors of the same quality wool, in small amounts (approximately .12 oz. [3 g]) each or .33 oz. (10 g) total

* Use either a digital scale or a balance scale using weights.

This is an exercise in making a soft felt fabric, called prefelt, which is used for design purposes. To make this fabric, the shrinking stage is stopped before the wool has shrunk too much. The swatch should be strong enough to maintain its shape for cutting, but still be an open and pliable fabric for further entanglement with a wool base. Shapes cut from this sample can be used as inlaid design elements (such as in the Fun Shoulder Bags on page 49).

The use of prefelt motifs by nomadic peoples is one of the most important traditional methods of producing controlled patterns with limited materials, and it is still readily employed today (see page 121, Shōsō-in and Iranian carpets.)

1

2

3a

1

The bamboo mat used here is the correct size for this sample. For other sized mats, or if using bubble wrap, use a permanent marker to draw a rectangle measuring approximately 10½" x 13" (26.5 x 33 cm) in the center of the mat. Inside the lower one-third of the rectangle, place three or four thin layers of one color, rotating 90 degrees for each layer. Repeat for the next two colors in the same manner in the center and upper-third of the rectangle. Make sure the edges of each color overlap slightly, resulting in an even thickness of wool throughout.

2

Cover the wool with a net and thoroughly wet it with hot felting solution (but not so hot that it can't be touched). With a plastic bag over one hand, smooth out any air pockets between the layers.

3a

Carefully remove the net and work the wet edges by sweeping the extending fibers back toward the outline with your fingertips. It is not necessary to fold them over onto themselves. To extend the size of a mat, place a plastic bag on the end closest to you. (If you are using a mat larger than the sample and have room between the wool edge and the end of the mat, extra plastic is not necessary.) Place a small-diameter rolling rod (1" [2.5 cm]) as a solid core, and roll up the mat, wool, and plastic bag around the rod. Wind rubber bands on each end to secure the bundle.

3b

Wrap the rolled bundle tightly in a towel in the same direction as before (see step 10 on page 22). The towel will absorb excess felting solution pressed out during rolling, and protect your bare arms from the rough surface of the mat or bubble wrap.

3b

4a

4b

5

6

7

8

4a |

Start rolling, from your fingertips toward your elbows and back toward your fingertips (equaling one count). Roll the bundle for fifty counts. (See page 123 for Healthy Postures in Feltmaking.) Open up the bundle and reroll it from the opposite end, then roll for another fifty counts. Flip over the sample and roll fifty counts lengthwise once more from each end, opening and repositioning the rod each time. Watch the fabric slowly shrink and tighten up.

4b |

Open the bundle and flip the prefelt over, then turn it 90 degrees so it lies sideways. Continue rolling and repeat the procedure described in step 4a. Apply hot felting solution when needed.

5 |

Once the thin fabric feels more solid, remove the bamboo mat and wind the felt piece directly around the rod. Wrap it well in a towel and roll it another fifty counts. Repeat this step several times.

6 |

The sample is ready when the width (here, the horizontal stripes) is 20 to 25 percent narrower than the outline. If your sample has not shrunk enough, at this stage in the process (and only now) the fabric can be rolled like a ball between your palms for thirty counts; this motion will shrink it further.

NOTE: It is critical not to overshrink the sample. Stop working upon reaching the 20 to 25 percent change in size, or you may have difficulty joining it to the base wool in subsequent projects.

7 |

Spread the sample on the mat to determine if the piece is the right size. If not, repeat step 6 several times until the proper size is achieved. Rinse the piece well in warm water, wring it in a towel, iron and reshape it into a straight edge rectangle, and leave it to air dry.

8 |

In this sample, the zigzag border design and letters were cut out with sharp scissors and then felted into a background of base wool (white wool carded with pieces of linen thread). During the shrinking stage the design becomes enmeshed in the base wool and adheres without glue or stitching, a good example of how felting can be used instead of appliqué techniques. NOTE: If you find that you have accidentally shrunk a prefelt piece too much, let the prefelt dry, and then try striking the back of the fabric with a hand carder. Raising fibers before cutting out a design will ensure that the roughed-up side attaches better to the wool base.

UNDERSTANDING THE CHARACTERISTICS of certain wools, and how to make a custom quality blend, will help you create the right expression for a work and avoid disappointing results. Making small project samples and comparing different wool qualities can serve as valuable notes to refer back to as you begin transforming wool into wonderful pieces of art and hand-crafted projects.

Breed Samples

MATERIALS
- Washed, carded wool (light gray romney top is used here), .5 oz. (15 g) per breed sample*

* Use either a digital scale or a balance scale using weights.

It is easy to see the characteristics of different sheep breeds by comparing samples made of equal amounts of wool, under equal conditions. For beginning felters, making samples will teach you how fabric is formed from loose wool fibers as well as the principles of the technique. This exercise also offers practice in controlling the shape of the work.

1

2

3

1

With a permanent marker, draw a square 8" x 8" (20.5 x 20.5 cm) in the center of a bamboo mat (or sheet of bubble wrap.) Before starting, divide the wool top into eight equal sections to help keep track of the material. In the vertical direction, lay down one section in overlapping tufts, just to the edge of the outline. To do this, hold a section in your right or left hand and draw the ends of the fibers out by grasping them with your opposite hand between four fingers and the palm; gently pull the fibers straight out in small, sheer quantities, and lay them directly onto the mat. NOTE: Make sure all areas of this first layer are of equal thickness and the fibers don't extend over the outline of the square.

2

Rotate the mat 90 degrees; then lay another full section of overlapping tufts in the vertical direction (and perpendicular to the first layer). Continue rotating the mat after each layer, until the four top sections are in place. Press the wool with dry hands to stabilize the layers, keeping them within the boundaries.

3

Cover the layers with a net, completely moisten them with felting solution, and press out any air pockets between the layers. Remove the net. Repeat step 2 for the four remaining sections. NOTE: Although the wetted fibers have now stretched beyond the outline of the square, lay the next four layers of dry wool just to the edge of the outline.

4

5

6a

6b

6c

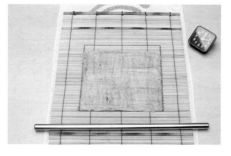

4 |

Stabilize the wool with a net and thoroughly wet all eight layers with hot felting solution; then remove the net. Fold over all four edges carefully to make the 8" x 8" (20.5 x 20.5 cm) square. Lightly wet the folded edges to keep them in place, then rub them briefly, if necessary, with a plastic bag over your hand.

5 |

Place a 1/2" (2.5 cm) -diameter rod at one edge of the mat, then carefully and lightly roll up the mat with the sample inside; avoid making deep wrinkles. Secure the mat tightly at both ends with rubber bands to prevent the roll from opening. NOTE: After the first rolling session the sample will start to felt and you will be able to roll it more tightly, but take it easy in the beginning.

6a |

Next, tightly roll the bundle in a towel, continuing in the same direction. The towel lessens the irritation on your forearms during the rolling process and absorbs any excess felting solution.

6b |

Set the timer for two minutes and start rolling lightly but quickly (approximately eighty to ninety counts per minute). NOTE: A single roll count constitutes the entire rolling movement, from fingertips to elbows and back to fingertips. It is easier to exert more pressure on the bundle from your upper shoulders and your natural bodyweight rather than using only your arm muscles (see page 129 for the proper felting position).

6c |

Stop after two minutes, open the mat, and check to see that the sample has shrunk in the vertical direction. (The direction in which you roll the sample will cause the fibers laid in that same direction to migrate and entangle.) In order to maintain a perfect square, flip the sample over and rotate it 90 degrees. Roll it back up, and repeat step 6b for the next two-minute session. Repeat again, then wet the sample with hot felting solution. Repeat the timed rolling and rotations for a total of twelve minutes (six two-minute sessions). Apply slightly more pressure after each rolling session, as the wool fibers blend into a fabric. NOTE: During the rolling, bear in mind that the goal is a square. Once a sample, or felt piece, has been rolled several times, you should not assume that rolling is always done in alternate directions. This is not only a sample exploring the quality of a particular wool, but it is also an exercise in achieving a proper square shape.

7

Intermittently, fold the sample diagonally to check that it is square. If it isn't, roll the sample in the direction of the longer side during the next session. Do not work the sample by rote; instead, decide which is the better direction to roll in to maintain a good shape. Roll the last two sessions without the mat, using only the rod, sample, and towel, and securing the project with rubber bands at both ends on the outside of the towel. During the felting process, once the wool has become a somewhat tighter fabric, the mat is not necessary and will actually slow down the speed of shrinking.

8

After twelve minutes, this romney sample will have shrunk approximately 18 percent. Check to see if the wool you are using for your sample has shrunk from its original size. Rinse out the soap in lukewarm water, and roll and wring out the excess moisture in a towel or spin dry. Reshape the sample by pulling the edges and steam ironing, then leave it to air dry.

7

8

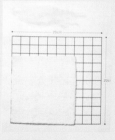
Merino 64s top

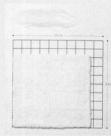
Crossbred 58s top

Down breed batt

ASSESSING A BREED SAMPLE

Once the "twelve minute" breed sample is done and dried, it is time to assess if this is a good fiber for feltmaking. First of all, be assured that there is no such thing as a perfectly felted sample. For example, if the rolling time were increased, the sample would continue to shrink. The six two-minute rolling-session limit is an arbitrary stopping point in deciding if a wool is useful in feltmaking. The time period is a benchmark for comparing various types of wool, felted under the same conditions.

Several things will happen during that time to help determine the following: 1) the general image of the felted wool, 2) the felting speed (fast felting or slow felting), 3) the approximate percentage of shrinkage (from fluffy fiber to felted fabric), and 4) how the fibers blend together. In the case of the light gray Romney wool used here, the color became denser after felting, and the overall felted fabric looked different than the unfelted, loose fibers.

The best way to keep track of these various wool samples is to start a "twelve minute" notebook that is large enough to hold all the samples and the accompanying notes.

THIS BRIGHTLY COLORED and simply shaped pendant is a smart accessory to a winter sweater. After finishing the crescent-shaped pendant, string extra beads of felt, or other complementary material such as ceramics, onto the cord to create unique and interesting variations.

Crescent Pendants

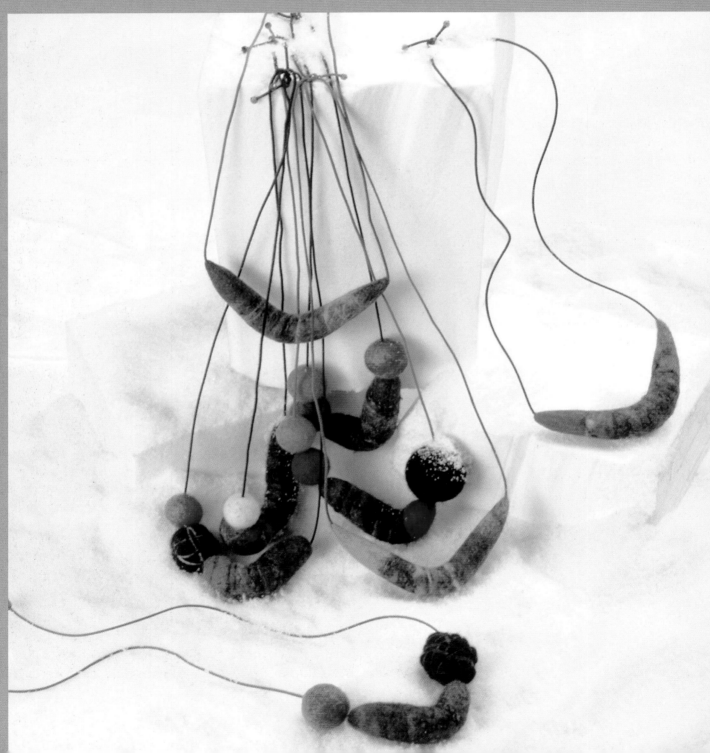

MATERIALS

- White merino 64s top for the core, approximately .33 oz. (10 g)*
- Dyed merino wool for surface pattern (minimal amount)
- Novelty yarn for decoration, 70 to 100 percent wool
- ¹/₁₆" (2 mm) –diameter linen cord (nylon core), 40" (1 m) long
- 2 glass beads with holes large enough for the cord, to finish each end of the necklace

* Use either a digital scale or a balance scale using weights.

1

For the core: Cut one 8" (20.5 cm) length of white merino top into two 4" (10 cm) lengths for core of bead. Slightly spread open one of the lengths and place it on the bamboo mat. Sprinkle it with hot felting solution. Place the middle of the cord in the center of the wool and roll them up together.

2a

Gently roll the wool and cord section inside the mat for twenty counts using light pressure.

2b

Slightly spread open the second length of white top, place the first wool-cord section inside, wet with felting solution, and roll them up tightly together. Repeat step 2a.

3

For the decorative design layer: Using two or three colors of your choice, wrap the white core tightly in multiple thin layers of colored wool until the white core is no longer visible. Moisten the surface with a small amount of felting solution and roll it lightly in the mat for twenty counts.

4

Wrap novelty yarn very tightly around the shape and secure the ends of the yarn by slipping them under itself. Roll the shape in the mat horizontally for fifty counts. Then rub it vertically between your palms for fifty counts.

5a

To avoid elongation of the shape that occurs when pushing down on the project, use the fingers to simultaneously pull both ends of the cord out while forcing the wool back towards the center of the cord.

2b

3

1

2a

4

5a

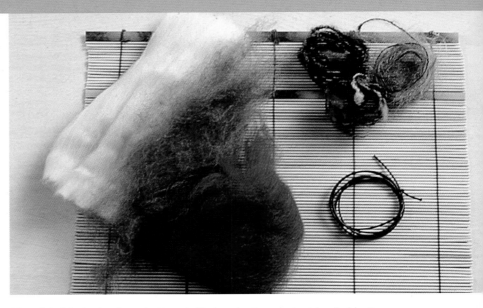

Materials (clockwise from bottom left): two to three color-blended batts
(see pages 109 to 110 on carding), cut white top for core, novelty yarns, and cord.

5b

5c

5b

To shape the crescent, hold your hands at a slanted position and work the edges toward the center of the core while rolling on the mat. Continue rolling to form a thick center and thinner ends. Apply additional soap or hot felting solution as necessary. Roll and shrink the crescent until it is as hard as a rubber ball.

5c

To help form the shape, rub it in the curve of your soapy palm. Rinse well in hot water. Spin it or roll it in a towel to remove any excess moisture. Reshape it into a perfect crescent moon and leave it to dry.

6

To finish the necklace: Thread one end of the dry cord through a glass bead. Snip off the end of the cord, as it will have frayed during the process, and secure the bead with instant bonding glue. Repeat for the opposite end. Knot the cord at the appropriate length and enjoy your new accessory. Optional finish: Using a thick needle, add some colorful felt beads on either side of the pendant before gluing the glass beads to the cord ends.

THROUGH THE WONDERS OF FELTMAKING, it is easy to join separate
objects together to make a sweet, two-toned flower. You can use a single small
flower as a brooch, or make a dozen for a flower bouquet or vase arrangement.
Adding an extra-long stem to a flower allows it to be a worn as a choker.
This is a very interesting technique that starts by making felt around a stone
to help create the hollow flower form.

Flower Bouquets

MATERIALS

- Dyed 58s to 64s top, two colors, .12 oz. (3 g) each, for multicolor petals*
- Dyed 58s to 64s top, .12 oz. (3 g) for 5" (13 cm) –long stem
- Dyed top or yarn for pistils (the delicate strands in the flower center), minimal amount
- Small round object for forming flower head (i.e. smooth rock or hard rubber ball)

* Use either a digital scale or a balance scale using weights.

1

2

3

4

5

1

This photo shows an assortment of dyed wool top for flower petals and stems: a rock, a foam ball, and a hard ball for forming the flower, and several finished, felt flowers. In the following steps, the smooth rock is used as the form.

2

To shape the pistils: Yarn pistils can be sewn on after completing the flower, but here the pistils are connected to the flower center. Separate a couple of strips of wool tops, in the desired pistil color, about ½" (1.3 cm) longer than the circumference of the stone, and about as thick as a toothpick. Moisten the pistil with felting solution and roll it inside the bamboo mat until it has felted into a cord. Repeat to make as many pistils as desired.

3

Wrap the wet pistils vertically around the wet stone as securely as possible, with ends overlapping, and set aside.

4

To make the multicolor petals: Divide each of the two petal colors evenly into four sections (eight sections total). Each section should then be turned into small fluffy piles (approximately 4" [10 cm] in diameter); be sure to alternate the direction of the layers horizontally and vertically (see Simple Balls and Things, page 18). Repeat for all eight sections. Starting with the inner petal color, wrap the four piles, one by one, evenly and tightly around the rock and pistils. (It is easier to roll the rock in the wool on a tabletop rather than working in the air.) Moisten the wool with felting solution between layers and squeeze out any air. Try to roll each layer as tightly and evenly spread over the rock as possible.

5

Wrap three of the outer petal color sections tightly around the stone, reserving the last section for step 10. Apply felting solution. Rub the palms of your hands with a bar of soap and begin lightly massaging the wool-covered rock, feeling for uniformity of thickness. (It is also helpful to place the rock in the contained corner of a plastic bag and rub from the outside so the wool doesn't stick to your hands.) Continue rubbing for four to five minutes or until the original shape of the rock becomes more defined and there are no wrinkles on the

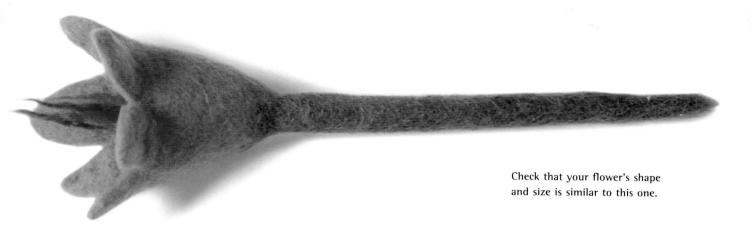

Check that your flower's shape and size is similar to this one.

outside when the felted surface is lightly squeezed. This is known as a pinch-test. (For more information, see page 133.)

6

To make the stem: To determine the suitable thickness of wool tops for the stem, twist the dyed top 1½ times while pulling it in opposite directions between your hands. This thickness will roughly equal the final felted stem. Place this section of the wool onto the bamboo mat, leaving approximately 2" to 3" (5 to 7.5 cm) of the wool off the edge. This end portion will be joined to the flower part, so keep it as dry as possible by holding it in your fingers while rolling the mat.

7

Sprinkle only the portion of the stem resting on the mat with felting solution, and gently roll it in the mat ten times to make a ropelike stem. Open the mat and sprinkle more felting solution or rub some soap onto the stem; keep working until the stem stiffens and, if shaken, will not droop over. NOTE: It is easier to work the stem before attaching the flower part, so keep at it by applying more pressure to the mat.

8

Pulling the dry end wool fibers open, work toward the tighter center, or neck of the stem, and distribute the wool evenly to form an ice cream–cone shape.

9

For the flower and stem sections: Place the felted "stone bud" vertically into the cone and tightly pull the dry, loose wool over and around it.

10

Wrap the bud firmly with the reserved layer of outer wool, encasing the top of the stem as well. Sprinkle it with felting solution and gently massage down from the neck of the stem toward the bud. (Placing the project in a plastic bag makes the rubbing easier.) Continue felting the flower for approximately ten minutes or until the wool forms a tight skin around the bud and is joined securely to the stem. Roll it inside the bamboo mat if needed.

7

8

9

6

10

Long-stem flower chokers

11

12

13

14

11

With sharp scissors, carefully cut an opening in the top of the flower and search for the pistils. Cut each pistil in half, and then position them out of the way. Cut the slit across the top just deep enough to remove the rock. Continue cutting the fabric until you create the desired number of petals.

12

Gently pull the pistils off the wall of the flower, but leave them attached at the base. Using soap and a plastic bag, begin to massage the individual petals, stretching them into a nice shape. To work the tiny pistils, use your bare fingertips until the pistils become stiff.

13

Between hand-felting sessions, roll the flower briefly inside the mat (approximately ten times). Repeat hand felting until the flower has crisp features and its petals show slight color blending between the layers.

14

Once the flower is completed, rinse well and blot the excess moisture with a towel. Reshape the flower and leave it to dry. NOTE: To make a flower hat band or choker, start with a 44" (112 cm) stem length and shrink it about 20 percent.

Flower and bird hat pins

ARTISTS OFTEN USE FOAM RUBBER as a core to make lightweight, solid objects. For this project, foam-rubber cushion material is used for the core. The doggie's nose, tongue, and ears will be stitched on later using complementary materials, rather than trying to incorporate these finer features from the start.

During the feltmaking process, corners tend to become rounded, and as a result, rounder forms make easier felting projects. Any sharp edges and inner angles should be exaggerated when cutting out the foam-rubber form. Start with small, simple animal shapes, such as a mouse, a swallow, or a goldfish. It is important to use finer wool that will tighten and felt quickly to encase the core.

Doggie Toys

MATERIALS
- Template (page 39)
- White merino 64s wool top for base, .5 oz. (15 g)
- Dyed merino 64s wool for design layer, two brown colors
- Foam rubber, 3⅛" to 4" (8.5 to 10 cm) thick
  (or glue foam cushions together for desired thickness)
- White knitting yarn; fine, soft 100 percent wool (avoid Super Wash)
- Miniature bell (preferably encased in plastic)
- Beads and leather scraps for eyes, nose, tongue, and collar
  (NOTE: small pieces are not suitable for toys for children under three years old)

1

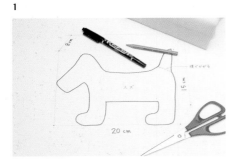

2

3

4

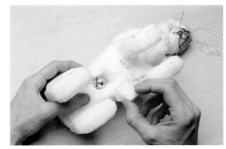

1

Enlarge the template shown on page 39 and draw it on 6" x 8" (15 x 20.5 cm) paper. Cut out the pattern.

2

Using the pattern, draw an outline on both sides of the block of foam rubber.

3

Squeeze the foam rubber while cutting and trimming the outline of the dog form. Cut out the dog's tail from a scrap of foam rubber.

5

6

4

First, carve a rough shape using scissors and a utility knife. Then, to form the underbelly, cut out at least one-third of the core between the front and hind legs. Keep in mind that the space will again narrow as you wrap wool around the limbs in step 7.

5

Sew the foam-rubber tail to the body with several big stitches.

6

In the dog's underbelly, cut out a hole larger than the bell. Place the bell inside, and cover it with a small piece of foam rubber. Sew the piece back in place.

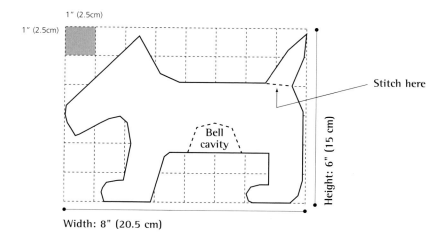

1" (2.5cm)

1" (2.5cm)

Stitch here

Bell cavity

Height: 6" (15 cm)

Width: 8" (20.5 cm)

7 |

Wrap the foam rubber completely with thin layers of 64s white merino wool.

8 |

Wind the white yarn snugly over the base wool and around the areas where the wool may have difficulty adhering, such as limbs, joints, and under the chin.

9 |

Spread out a towel and place a bamboo mat on top. Position the dog form on top of the mat and add more thin layers of white 64s, alternating the layers horizontally and vertically. Sprinkle felting solution between every layer, and squeeze out the air to stabilize the fibers.

10 |

Continue adding thin layers of wool, creating a uniform thickness, until the yarn is completely hidden. For narrower, more difficult spots such as the neck and shoulder joints, feet, and tail, cut the wool fibers to 1⅜" to 1½" (3.5 to 4 cm) lengths. NOTE: Applying a shorter length of wool to these areas is better than continuously wrapping longer fiber tufts. In general, shorter fibers make the felting process faster.

11 |

Select one of the brown wools and a coat pattern for the dog. Layer the brown wool over the white base.

9

10

11

7

8

12

13

14

15

16

12

Repeat step 9 with the brown wool, adding felting solution or extra soapsuds between the layers when necessary. NOTE: Be sure to completely cover the white wool base, which can easily be mistaken for suds.

13

Using the second blended wool, make spot patterns on the dog's coat and face.

14

Start massaging slowly and gently at first. Be careful that the layers of wool do not shift out of place. If any white wool starts to show through, immediately add more brown wool over that area to conceal it. (It will be harder to do so later.) Using slippery plastic bags on your hands will make the rubbing easier.

15

Take care not to overwork the felt. The goal here is to create a well-felted skin around the form while preventing the shrinking wool from deforming the core shape. When the surface is smooth and has hardened enough so that each fiber's direction cannot be distinguished, rinse well in warm water, spin in clothes dryer or salad spinner, and leave it to dry. After your dog is dry, check for any areas that may still be slightly fluffy and not well felted. If you find any areas that still need work, apply hot felting solution and continue massaging until fully felted, then rinse again and dry as above.

16

Sew on the nose, tongue, and ears. Embroider a smiley mouth and add a leather collar.

WHY NOT MAKE A MOUSE with natural color wool? Or dye the little pet after completing it in white. Since this is such a small felt object, shorter, finer wool fibers are used. In earlier projects, did you have problems with felted wrinkles sticking out? Well, in this project, that's exactly the goal!

Mouse

MATERIALS

- Dyed 58s to 64s top, .25 to .33 oz. (7 to 10 g)*
- Beads for eyes, two (NOTE: small pieces are not suitable for toys for children under three years old)
- Stiff thread for whiskers, such as black linen thread
- Embroidery thread for ears, beige or pink

  * Use either a digital scale or a balance scale using weights.

1

2

3a

3b

4a

1 |

Start this project from the mouse's tail. Measure a small amount of wool about 7" (18 cm) long and the appropriate thickness for a mouse's tail. To check the thickness, twist it $1\frac{1}{2}$ times while pulling on the wool top. This is approximately what the felted tail will look like. Leaving $2\frac{3}{8}$" (6 cm) outside a bamboo mat, roll the wool inside the mat following the flower stem steps on page 35. Continue rolling until it becomes a stiff, tapered tail.

2 |

Using the ball-making technique (see page 18), form a body by wrapping wool, horizontally and vertically, around the thicker, dry end of the tail. Sprinkle felting solution as needed.

3a |

Use your fingers to make a general outline of the mouse body by softly massaging it into shape. If the body appears too small (it will shrink as you work the surface), immediately wrap more thin layers of dry wool around the form and sprinkle it with more felting solution. Pinch, pull, and rub to form the mouse's snout with your fingertips.

3b |

Pinch and pull the ears up while the body is still soft and pliable.

4a |

Continue to massage the mouse body. Sprinkle more felting solution, if needed, to make the rubbing easier and prevent the wool from sticking to your fingers.

4b |

Work your fingertips to emphasize the ears, mouth, and curved back of the body.

5 |

When the direction of the outermost layers of fibers is indistinguishable and the mouse feels firmly felted, rinse well, then spin or squeeze out the excess moisture in a towel, reshape, and leave it to dry. NOTE: It may be hard to make a good shape on your first attempt, so try several times to achieve a lifelike size and shape.

Cute teddy bear friends

6 |

For the eyes, sew beads tightly to either side of the snout, causing a slight indentation and a more realistic facial expression.

7 |

Accentuate the shape of each ear by embroidering the inner area with lighter-colored embroidery floss. Alternatively, apply a tiny bit of colored wool by needling it in place (For more on needle felting, see page 132.)

8 |

For the whiskers, sew stiff lengths of linen thread into the snout and knot them on either side of the snout to secure their position. Embroider the tip of the snout to create a cute nose.

4b

5

6

7

8

Just for
you

BABY Bee Boots

IN FELTMAKING IT IS PREFERABLE to use the same wool for both the design and base layer of the work because they will have the same felting speed. Here, however, merino wool is used for the base and black sections of the booties, and over-dyed light gray romney is used for the yellow section. Corriedale is also suitable for this project. Since this is a small object, finer, shorter wool is usually recommended. Alternatively, longer fibers such as romney could be cut into shorter lengths before using.

Be aware that in this project the instructions start with the outside yellow-and-black-stripe layers. The white base will keep the motif in place while felting; the booties are then turned inside out when they are nearly finished. This technique gives a nicer surface to the fabric, and is especially useful for projects with more detailed designs. (Design variations of the bumblebee booties are suggested in the photo at left.)

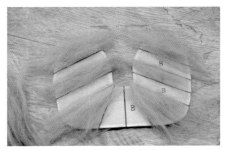

1

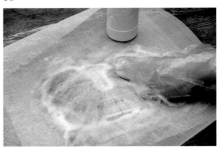

2

3a

3b

4a

MATERIALS
- Template (page 47)
- White 58s to 64s top for base, .88 oz. (25 g)
- Dyed wool for the decorative pattern, .33 oz. (10 g)*
- Cord for laces, 36" (90 cm) cut in two
- Glass beads for shoelace end, four

* Use either a digital scale or a balance scale using weights.

1

Enlarge the template shown on page 47 and draw the pattern on cardboard. Cut out the form and tape around the exposed edges. Draw lines for the stripes on both sides of the form, and mark the sections to identify the colors. Divide the white base wool and the two pattern colors in half for the front and back of the booties. NOTE: The booties are joined at the start and are cut in two when they are half-felted to make the pair.

2

Place the form onto a slightly larger sheet of plastic. Take one-half of the yellow wool (cut to 1" (3 cm) lengths if necessary) and lay it out, a little at

4b

5a

a time, within the inner stripes and just to the edges of the form and toe areas, on the upper side only. NOTE: Do not lay all the wool out at once, as it will be too thick.

3a

Place a net over the wool and sprinkle it with felting solution. Using a plastic bag over your hand, gently massage the yellow wool until it lies flat (the wool ends will relax and extend slightly over the edge of the form when wet.) Remove the net and add more thin layers of yellow wool until the pattern areas for yellow are evenly covered and half the yellow wool used up. Lay the net down and thoroughly wet the wool again, as above.

3b

Take another plastic sheet and place it over the form. Carefully flip the bundle over and remove the first plastic sheet. While gently pulling at the yellow wool extending from the underside, fold it up and over the form onto the corresponding yellow areas. Do this for all the yellow sections. Using the remaining half of the yellow wool, repeat step 2, making thin layers and wetting them with felting solution. Continue until the yellow areas are covered. Flip over the booties again. Tightly pull the loose ends of the yellow wool up and over the edges. NOTE: Make sure the yellow wool does not creep onto the areas reserved for the black wool.

1" (2.5 cm)

1" (2.5 cm)

Toe   Toe

Black

Yellow

Height: 6" (15 cm)

Width: 9¾" (25 cm)

Cut here/Boot opening

5b

5c

5d

6

7

4a |

Fill in the black areas with multiple layers of the black wool. Repeat step 3a with the black wool.

4b |

Flip over the booties and continue as in step 3b until the motif layer is completed.

5a |

Take one half of the white top and divide it into four equal sections. Holding the wool with your left hand, pull small amounts of wool out with your right hand, and begin to add multiple thin layers of wool on top of the black-and-yellow design.

5b |

Lay the white wool base in alternating layers, both vertically and horizontally, turning the plastic sheet 90 degrees after each layer is completed.

5c |

Cover the booties with a net and wet them thoroughly with warm felting solution. Remove the net, lay down a plastic sheet, and gently flip over the wool and form. Pull the extending wool from underneath up and over the form to make a tight edge. NOTE: Maintain the resist form exactly.

5d |

Repeat the process of positioning the remaining half of the white wool. Make four layers as in step 5a, and then repeat steps 5b and 5c. Continue until no striped color is visible.

6 |

With plastic bags on hands, gently massage the surface of the booties from the outside in, in the direction of the last layer of base. Be very gentle at first, then gradually increase the pressure as the surface of the wool begins to tighten up (about ten minutes per side). Add hot felting solution as needed. Cup the edges in your hands and massage them as well.

7 |

Do a pinch-test to determine if the fabric is ready to be cut (see page 133.) If areas of the fabric appear soft (the individual fibers are pulling away and are not enmeshed, and the layers have not joined as one), keep massaging another few minutes on each side. Apply very hot felting solution to encourage the shrinking process.

8a

8b

9

10

11

12

13

8a

Using sharp scissors, carefully cut the center of the pattern to separate the booties. Gently remove the form pieces, taking care not to disturb the inner design. NOTE: Check if the stripes have successfully attached to the base. If not, leave the cardboard forms inside, and continue felting the outside with your fingertips, adding more pressure for a few more minutes on each side.

8b

Measure, mark with a pin, and cut a 1⅜" (3.5 cm) notch along the crease from the top front side of each bootie.

9

Turn each bootie right side out and sprinkle it with hot felting solution. Massage any wrinkles out with your hands. NOTE: If any white base shows through, cut the appropriate color wool into short lengths and reinforce the area by massaging small pieces in place.

10

Place both booties lengthwise on a bamboo mat, and roll the booties and the mat completely around a plastic pipe, or dowel, as a core. Next, wrap the rolled bundle in a towel and roll it lightly for about fifty counts.

11

Spread open the booties widthwise, folding in the notched edges. This will open the creased lines formed in step 10, and the folds will fade away in the next rolling session. Moisten the booties with felting solution and roll them in the mat for another fifty counts.

12

Repeat steps 10 and 11, rolling the booties in opposite directions and getting rid of any fold lines. Check to see if the booties are the same size and shape. If not, use your hands to stretch and pull them into the correct form, applying soap to the surface, if needed. Roll and shrink the booties to the desired size.

13

To strengthen the notched edges, cover your hand with a plastic bag, pinch the area with your thumb and forefinger, and evenly rub these areas back and forth. Stretch the toe areas to make them more comfortable for little toes. To finish the booties, rinse them well in warm water and spin dry. Use a steam iron to press and reshape the booties. Stuff crumpled newspaper inside each bootie, shape, and leave them to dry. Use an awl to punch six holes for the laces, three on either side of the notch, about ⅜" (1 cm) from the edge. Lace up using a ¹⁄₁₆" (2 mm) ribbon or cord. Glue or stitch beads to the ends or knot the laces.

A SEAMLESS SHOULDER BAG? What may seem impossible is possible through the magic of feltmaking (and the use of a cardboard barrier, called a reserve). To learn more about seamless, three-dimensional felting, let's make a simple, but handy shoulder bag with decorative tails, a secret pocket, and a sturdy strap. You'll even have the opportunity to incorporate that leftover yarn from last year's sweater to enhance the motif.

Fun Shoulder Bags

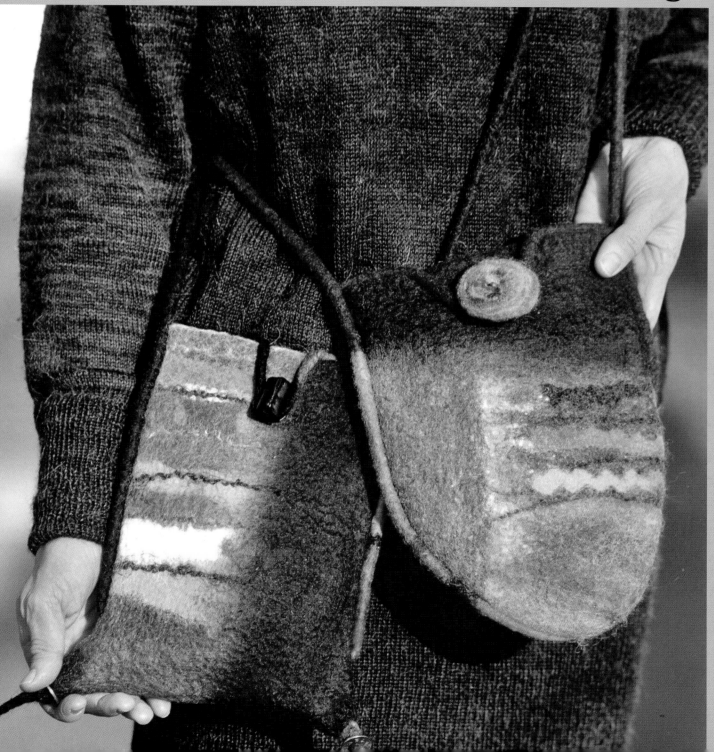

MATERIALS

- Template (page 51)
- Dyed 58s to 64s wool top for base, 3.17 to 3.5 oz. (90 to 100 g)
- Dyed wool top for decorative design layer, .18 to .53 oz. (5 to 15 g)*
- Mohair or other novelty yarns for finer decoration, 70 to 100 percent wool content
- Color prefelt and/or woolen fabric (for cut-out designs), small amounts in various colors

* Use either a digital scale or a balance scale using weights.

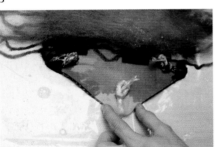

1 |

Enlarge, draw, and cut the template shown on page 51 from cardboard, then tape the edges. (As with the bootie project on page 46, work begins with the outer motif of the bag; thus, the motif elements are placed directly on the form, followed by the base wool to keep the intricate motif in place.) To create the decorative design layer, place the form on a plastic sheet. Lay out a design with the yarn directly onto the form. Keep in mind that the bag design will be viewed from all directions. If the design is a continuous one, the yarn should be long enough to continue around to the back. Cut out the motif pieces from prefelt or loosely woven wool fabric and lay them on top of the yarn, or vice versa. NOTE: Remember that any element placed directly on the form will be the most exposed motif when the bag is turned right side out. Sprinkle it with felting solution to keep the design stable.

2 |

For the decorative tails: Separate a 6" (15 cm) length of dyed top for each different color tail. Separate each length again, widthwise, so the tail is not too thick. Since the tail will be joined to the base wool, keep approximately ³/₄" (2 cm) of one end dry. Dip the remaining length into felting solution, wrap it in plastic wrap, and secure it by loosely knotting the wrapped end, leaving only

the dry end of fibers sticking out. Trim the end to make it straight, as shown, or keep it as is. NOTE: After the bag has been felted, the tails will be finished by rolling them between the palms of your hands. All the designs elements must be on top of the form and will eventually be covered by the base wool. Nothing should hang off the form or it will get caught up in the base wool layering and not be able to be turned inside out. (Because the long tails are partially wrapped in plastic from the start, only their "roots" will be felted in.)

3 |

Lay each prepared wrapped and knotted tail onto its designated corner, with its dry end temporarily hanging off the edge. As shown in the photo, divide the dry end in half. Fold half of the dry fibers back on the side with the tail (the other half will be tucked under the cardboard corner and felted into the design on the back side). Wet the other half with felting solution to keep it in place.

4a |

For the final design layer: To add a touch more color to the design, place several very thin layers of complementary-color wool on top of the first motif elements. These may run off the edge of the form to continue onto the back side. Very little wool is needed here; too much wool will make the final bag fabric thick and clumsy. Remember to leave some areas free of design so the base color of

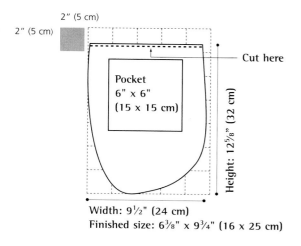

2" (5 cm)

2" (5 cm)

Pocket
6" x 6"
(15 x 15 cm)

Cut here

Height: 12⅝" (32 cm)

Width: 9½" (24 cm)
Finished size: 6⅜" x 9¾" (16 x 25 cm)

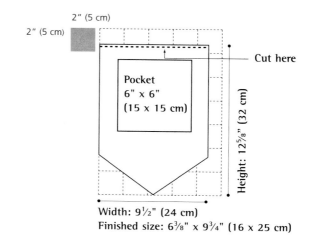

2" (5 cm)

2" (5 cm)

Pocket
6" x 6"
(15 x 15 cm)

Cut here

Height: 12⅝" (32 cm)

Width: 9½" (24 cm)
Finished size: 6⅜" x 9¾" (16 x 25 cm)

the bag is visible. Cover the wool with a net and completely wet it with warm felting solution, eliminating any air or wrinkles. Remove the net.

4b |

Cover the wool with a plastic sheet and carefully turn over the form. Remove the top plastic sheet.

4c |

Starting with the design yarn, tightly pull it around the form and overlap the ends to create a continuous design; wet to keep it in place. Check that the tails are still well positioned and the dry ends are now wetted and spread over the corner. Lay down the prefelt motif next. Finally, tautly pull the underside decorative design wool up and over the edges of the form, and fill in the corresponding areas following the design.

5 |

For the bag, strap, and pocket: Weigh out 3.17 oz. (90 g) of the wool top for the base of the bag. Be aware that this amount includes covering not only the bag but also the strap and pocket quantities. To determine the width of the strap (about ⅜" [1 cm]), separate and twist a narrow section (approximately ¼ to ⅓ of top) between your fingers, a maximum of 1½ times. Separate this amount carefully down the entire length of the wool. A sturdy strap needs to shrink at least 20 percent in length, so add 20 percent to the final length to

allow for the desired shrinkage. Set aside the strap wool for step 19; the excess should be enough for the pocket in step 9. NOTE: It is impossible to weigh these amounts at the start because it will not give you the length you need for the strap. Now that you have the separated amounts, you can check their weights: the strap is approximately .5 oz. (15 g) and the pocket is approximately .33 oz. (10 g).

6 |

To create the base layer for bag:
Carefully divide the rest of the base wool from step 5 in half for the front and back of the bag. Separate each half again into four parts, making a total of eight. Begin by placing a vertical layer over the prepared motif, laying the ends of the wool just to the edges of the form, but not beyond.

4b

4c

5

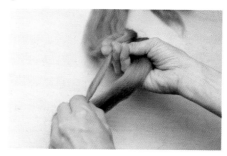

6

7

8a

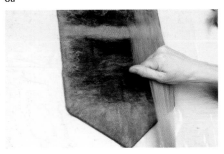

8b

9a

9b

7 |

Continue adding layers, rotating the form clockwise 90 degrees between layers. Cover the wool with the net and thoroughly wet the fibers with hot felting solution, pressing with your hands and squeezing out any air pockets. Check for even wetness and uniform thickness throughout. Remove the net, cover the wool with a plastic sheet, and gently turn it over. Carefully remove the top plastic sheet.

8a |

Pull the base wool ends from the underside up and over the edge and onto the form. Repeat step 7 to add four layers on this side. Then cover it with a plastic sheet and flip over the bag. Pull the underside base wool ends up and over the edge of the form. This is where the seamless trick starts. The cardboard form separates the top from the bottom fabrics but the edges will felt together, forming the connection.

8b |

Pull the corner fibers toward the center of the bag to eliminate excess bulk and wrinkles. Though you have now laid down all the bag wool, do not start massaging yet, as the hand felting begins when the pocket has been prepared in step 9. NOTE: The key concept of three-dimensional seamless felting is to employ a material, such as cardboard or plastic, to act as a reserve; this barrier prevents the front and back layers of the bag from joining together and allows only the wool ends along the edges to join into a fabric.

9a |

For the pocket: Instead of cardboard, use a thin sheet of plastic as the reserve. Cut a piece of plastic to measure 6" x 9" (15 x 23 cm). Center the pocket pattern on the backside of the bag, so that it extends 2" (5 cm) off the top edge of the bag. This extension will be folded back to reinforce and "hem" the top edge of the pocket.

9b |

Divide the pocket wool separated in step 5 into four equal parts and position them at 90 degree angles to each other over the reserve. Make sure each layer extends 1¼" (3 cm) and in even thickness beyond the edges of the plastic, so the edges of each layer can be joined directly to the body of the bag. Wet completely with felting solution.

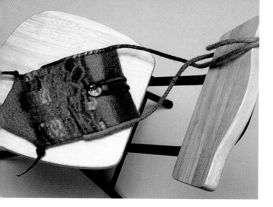

Finished Man-on-the-Moon bag

11a

11b

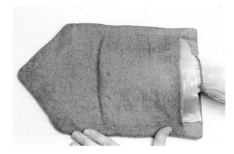

12

13

10

Fold over the plastic sheet (and wool) 1¼" (3 cm) below the top edge of the bag. Snip both corners of the pocket hem horizontally (just to the edge of the plastic reserve) and splay the wool out evenly with the fingertips to make better contact with the bag. Gently rub the folded portion flat. Cover the bag with a plastic sheet and flip over. Remove the top plastic sheet. Tightly pull up and over the form any wool extending from the pocket or underside. NOTE: Cut the extending section of plastic away but leave the rest of the reserve in place throughout the entire felting process to ensure that the pocket remains separate from the bag but felted at the pocket edges.

11a

Cover your hands with small, slippery plastic bags, then gently rub the form, starting in the direction of the last layer of fibers. Work from the edges toward the center of the bag. Do not make circular motions; stick to horizontal and vertical movements. Rub soap onto the plastic bags, if necessary, and consistently rub for ten minutes. (Set a timer to help you keep track).

11b

Flip over the bag again and begin gently massaging the pocket as well as the whole bag, including the outer edges. Evenly rub for ten minutes; then flip it over once more. Increasing the pressure from your fingertips so the inner design elements have a chance to adhere to the bag fabric, continue rubbing for an additional ten minutes per side. Check for signs that the layers are becoming one fabric.

12

The pocket area is composed of many layers (including the plastic reserve), so remember to gently rub the bag fabric inside the pocket as well. Leave the plastic reserve in place. While rubbing, check for any weak spots around the seam of the pocket. Add additional cut wool bits, if necessary, and continue to rub the area. Perform the pinch-test (see page 133) on both sides of the bag to check if all layers of wool have been successfully felted into one fabric. If weak areas appear, keep rubbing until the bag fabric feels strong.

13

With sharp scissors cut straight across the entire top of the bag, approximately ¼" (6 mm) from the edge. If desired, this piece can be used as the cord closure in the finishing stage, so do not discard it.

14a

14b

15

16

17

18

14a

Check to see that the design elements have adhered to the bag, and then carefully take out the cardboard form, gently turning the bag right side out. NOTE: If the design is not yet firmly felted into the base, sprinkle it with hot felting solution, and continue massaging before removing the form. Rub lightly to ensure that the design elements are joined well to the surface of the bag.

14b

Rub the edges of the inverted bag to remove any existing fold marks. The bag is now in the prefelted stage.

15

As the motif layer may still be delicate, invert the design again, then insert a small plastic bag fully into the opening to prevent the sides from adhering together during the rolling stage. Using a 1" (2.5 cm) -diameter rolling pipe, carefully roll up the bag in another plastic sheet. Roll the bundle in a towel to secure it well. Roll lightly for forty counts.

16

Unroll, stretch, and pull the bag into shape. Change the direction and roll up again for another forty counts. Repeat for all four sides. As the rolling continues, the fibers should gradually turn into a tight fabric.

17

Turn the bag right side out, position it on its side, reposition the edges, and repeat the rolling process.

18

Stop rolling when the bag is about 20 to 25 percent smaller than the cardboard form or when the design has fully adhered to the fabric base. Work the tails by rubbing them between your palms until they become strong cords. NOTE: If the tails are too fat, try separating them into two or three smaller tails and felt each separately. Remember to massage the felted bag opening between your thumb and fingers to round and strengthen the edges.

Bags with prefelt and woolen fabric patches, novelty yarn, and pencil-roving motifs

19a

For the shoulder strap: Take the strap top wool separated in step 5 and place it on the mat; sprinkle it with a little hot felting solution.

19b

Gently roll the entire length of wool inside the mat, ten counts per section, to form a soft cord.

20

Working section by section, tightly wind bits of leftover motif yarn and color wool around the soft cord. Gently roll it inside the mat. After completing the decorations along the entire length of the strap, start rolling again from end to end, gradually applying more pressure as the design starts to embed and the strap becomes stronger. Continue to roll until the length is 20 percent shorter than the start (work the entire length approximately eight to ten times.) Occasionally dip the cord into very hot water to promote shrinking. Using the bamboo mat, roll, stretch, and felt the short piece cut off the bag opening in step 13 into a strong closure cord.

21a

When the bag is finished, rinse the bag, strap, and short cord, and spin out any excess moisture. Steam iron and stretch the bag into a nice shape.

21b

Using needlenose pliers, straighten the edge opening.

22a

To finish the bag: Roll the damp strap in a clean bamboo mat to round out the shape, then leave the strap, closure cord, and bag to dry.

22b

Decide the position of the strap and sew it in place using invisible stitches, once from the front and again from the back. Shape the closure cord into a loop, and stitch the ends to the back of the bag. Sew a button onto the front, or make a small felt bead of your own design to complete the bag.

20

21a

21b

19a

19b

22a

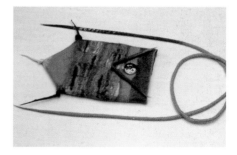

22b

MAKE A DOLL FOR A BEST FRIEND or fashion a doll in your own image! You can also make an interesting doll that is two-in-one: a sister on one side with a brother on the other. Once you start making dolls, it will be too much fun to stop!

Jack & Jill Dolls

MATERIALS

- Template (page 59)
- White merino 64s for base, .63 to .71 oz (18 to 20 g)
- Dyed merino for decoration motifs, such as skin, shoes, and clothes
- Small pieces of prefelt for added motif
- Color yarn, 70 to 100 percent wool content
- Two to six beads for eyes and buttons
- Four tiny buttons (optional)
- Polyester batting or old nylon stocking for stuffing
- 1/8" (3 mm) plain cardboard

1a

For the decorative design layer: Draw and cut your own doll figure, or enlarge one of the two templates shown on page 59. Trace it onto cardboard. Using clear tape, bind the edges of the cardboard cutout. With a permanent marker, draw the basic shirt, pants or skirt, shoes, hair, or any other decorative motifs onto both sides of the figure. Then choose small bits of wool color for these areas.

1b

Details such as collars, bows, and large polka dots can be made from prefelt. Arrange the finer details first by dipping them in felting solution and placing them on the figure, right side down. NOTE: Upon completion of the doll, finer facial expressions should be needle-felted (a dry technique using a special barbed needle) or embroidered using embroidery thread, colored wool, and beads. Otherwise, the wool marks made now may distort or "bleed" during the shrinking stage.

2a

Place the form onto a plastic sheet. Begin by placing very thin layers of cut, dyed wool over the motif areas that are going to be felted. For good results, add details in the following order: polka dots (only) of the shirt and the bows for shoes; the shirt color and the shoes; the socks, undershorts, and hair; and finally, the skin. Work in small areas, completing the shirt, shoes and other elements on both front and back sides before moving to the skin areas. NOTE: For design areas you do not need to alternate the direction of the layers. Use just enough design wool until the cardboard form is not visible.

2b

Once these colors have been filled in, cover the doll with a net, sprinkle it thoroughly with felting solution, and gently rub out any air pockets. Remove the net, cover the doll with another plastic sheet and flip it over. Remove the top plastic sheet and carefully fold over all the color wool onto the doll's back side, keeping the colors in the appropriate areas. NOTE: It is very important to fold the wool from the underside over tautly, following the shape of the pattern throughout the work.

1a

1b

2a

2b

3

4a

4b

5

6

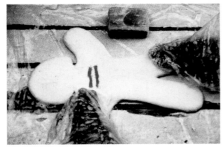

7a

3 |

When the back side is completely hidden under the layers of dyed wool, follow the wetting process, then turn it over. Using a fork to fold the wool ends over in the narrow areas may be helpful. Once the fluffy fibers are wet, check for any thin areas of the design. Lay more colored wool over these areas, if necessary, and gently rub them to an even thickness, wetting with felting solution.

4a |

For the base layer: Divide the white base wool in half, and reserve one half to use in step 5. Start laying the wool in thin multiple layers, alternating directions between layers. Cover the decorative motif completely, taking care to lay the wool just to the edges of the form.

4b |

For the narrow areas, such as the underarm, neck, and crotch, cut the wool into shorter lengths. Lay a plastic net over the base wool and sprinkle it generously with hot felting solution.

With a plastic bag over your hand, gently rub the net so that the felting solution spreads throughout the wool, pressing out any air at the same time. Sandwich the doll between two plastic sheets and turn it over.

5 |

Remove the top plastic sheet, then carefully pull and tautly fold over the white wool ends from underneath onto the form; repeat steps 4a and 4b with the remaining white wool.

6 |

Mark the front of the figure by rubbing a bit of yarn into the base layer. This will indicate where to cut the figure open later. Cover your hands with plastic bags, moisten the whole figure with felting solution, and begin to gently rub, using an outside-in motion. It is important not to allow the wool to slip off the form and mass at the edges. Work both sides of the figure for about ten minutes on each side. NOTE: Pay attention to the edges and make sure the rubbing is not distorting the shape of the cardboard form.

7a |

Do a pinch-test to check if the layers have entangled sufficiently, producing a soft piece of uniform cloth. Continue felting and applying hot felting solution if necessary to achieve this result.

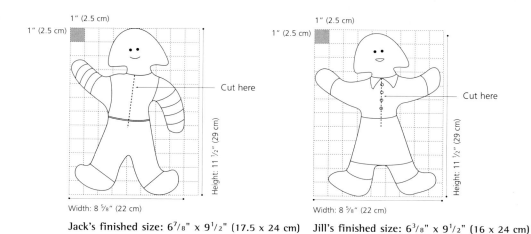

1" (2.5 cm)
1" (2.5 cm)

Cut here

Height: 11 ½" (29 cm)

Width: 8 ⅝" (22 cm)

1" (2.5 cm)
1" (2.5 cm)

Cut here

Height: 11 ½" (29 cm)

Width: 8 ⅝" (22 cm)

Jack's finished size: 6⅞" x 9½" (17.5 x 24 cm)   Jill's finished size: 6⅜" x 9½" (16 x 24 cm)

7b

Using a metal straightedge and a craft knife, carefully make a cut for the shirt opening. Begin approximately ⅜" (1 cm) from the base of the neck and end at the waist. Clip any remaining uncut fibers with a pair of scissors. NOTE: Take care to avoid cutting through the soft, wet cardboard; cut once with the knife and finish the job with the scissors.

7c

Cover your hand with a plastic bag and massage the edges of the opening.

8

Gently remove the cardboard pattern and turn the figure inside out, limbs first.

9a

Sprinkle the doll with felting solution, and rub the design gently with your plastic-covered hands.

9b

Use your fingers to stretch and smooth out any creased edges.

10a

Lay the doll on a plastic sheet, and using a narrow plastic pipe, tightly roll up the sheet and the doll together.

10b

Secure the roll by wrapping it in a damp towel.

10c

Roll twenty counts.

7b
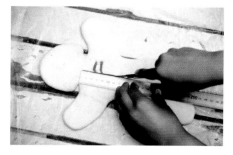

9b
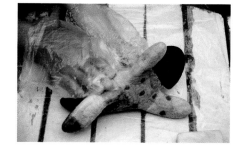

7c

10a

8

10b

9a

10c

ELEPHANT PRINCE MASK

Can you envision how this mask was made? For a first try, sketch the profile of the mask to fit into an $8^{1}/_{2}$" x 12" (22 x 31 cm) shape. Start with a 1 oz. (30 g) wool base. Keep in mind the fabric can be cut to alter the form during the shrinking process, or after drying. Follow steps 1 through 9b appropriately (here, the cut for the mask face is very wide, nearly half the form, allowing the fabric to be spread wide open). After the prefelt stage, find the proper location and cut the eye area. Then roll and harden (see steps 10a through 11). Finally, stretch the washed mask over a ball or hat form to round out the head, and leave to dry. Now it is ready for mounting on the wall, a costume, or for wearing on the ski slopes.

10d

Open the bundle and change the position of the felt figure in subsequent rolling sessions to maintain even proportions and avoid making creased edge lines. Start by rolling from head to toes and then roll in reverse, from toes to head. Roll from the left hand to the right and then reverse. Roll for twenty counts in each position. Check the slit opening between each count, stretching and straightening it with the fingers. Apply more pressure to the roll each time to increase the shrinkage.

11

Insert the rolling rod through the slit to stretch out and shape limbs, hands, and feet. When the felt figure has shrunk and hardened enough so that the design is embedded in the outer fabric and the direction of the last layer of fibers is unrecognizable, rinse it well, and spin or wring out excess moisture.

12

While the doll is still damp, stuff it with polyester batting or old stockings. Alternatively, use washed wool, dried beans, and cotton balls. NOTE: Polyester and nylon are better than cotton or wool because the doll can be easily washed and dried if soiled.

13

Align the shirt opening and stabilize it in place by basting two large Xs to keep it together; carefully stitch it closed with the appropriate color thread.

14

To finish the doll: Sew beads on for the eyes, and embroider the nose, mouth, and collar of the shirt. If using a felting needle, needle in the appropriate facial features with bits of colored wool or yarn. Be creative by adding additional hair, clothing, and accessories to make the doll unique. For example, dress Jill in a homemade felt skirt and make her a jump rope. Don't forget a leather belt and shoelaces for Jack.

10d

11

12

13

14

HATS! HATS! So many striking hats! From rolled-brim cowboy hats to royal pillboxes fit for a queen—whether a hat is handmade or comes from a factory, there are so many styles to choose from. Let's learn how to make a basic brimmed hat, and later on, a beret; soon you will be able to create all the head toppers and taxi stoppers you like. For feltmakers, this is a good way to practice felting techniques, including a simple stretched stiff brim. As with the shoulder bag project, decorative patterns for hats should be conceived with a 360 degree view in mind. This is truly a three-dimensional object, which will be seen from all angles.

A Lady's Hat

1

2a

2b

3

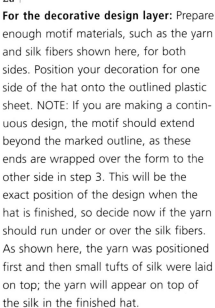

4a

MATERIALS
- Template (page 63)
- Dyed 58s for base: Color A) 1.41 to 1.76 oz. (40 to 50 g) for the outside (bright blue) Color B) 1.41 to 1.76 oz. (40 to 50 g) for the inside (pine green)
- Novelty yarn (70 to 100 percent wool content), silk fibers, and prefelt for decorative motif (optional)

1 |

Enlarge the template shown on page 63. Trace the pattern onto cardboard and cut out the shape. Bind the exposed edges with clear tape. Trace the form once again onto one sheet of plastic with a permanent marker.

2a |

For the decorative design layer: Prepare enough motif materials, such as the yarn and silk fibers shown here, for both sides. Position your decoration for one side of the hat onto the outlined plastic sheet. NOTE: If you are making a continuous design, the motif should extend beyond the marked outline, as these ends are wrapped over the form to the other side in step 3. This will be the exact position of the design when the hat is finished, so decide now if the yarn should run under or over the silk fibers. As shown here, the yarn was positioned first and then small tufts of silk were laid on top; the yarn will appear on top of the silk in the finished hat.

2b |

Cover the design with a net and lightly wet it with felting solution to stabilize the pieces.

3 |

Lay the cardboard form exactly over the plastic outline. Pressing with one hand on the form and being careful not to disturb the design on the back side, gently pull the underside motif ends up and onto the top of the cardboard. Fill in any missing pattern areas with motif bits, placing them in reverse fashion with finer details first and secondary motifs on top. Cover the form with a net, and sprinkle it with felting solution. Rub to evenly wet the motif and then remove the net. These two completed sides form the outer pattern of the hat. NOTE: This method of starting with the design and laying the base fibers on top helps to stabilize the hat and allows you to create a very detailed pattern, with less shifting of pattern during the felting process. (When the hat is completed, just turn it inside out to expose the design.)

4a |

For the hat base color A: Make sure there are no motif elements hanging off the sides of the form before proceeding. Divide color A top into eight equal sections (four per side). Each section equals the allotted amount per layer.

4b |

Take one section of wool top and start placing thin overlapping segments, vertically, similar to roof shingling, directly over the motif. Make sure the layers touch the edges of the form. Rotate the plastic sheet 90 degrees clockwise before starting the next layer. Repeat with the remaining three layers. NOTE: Be cautious when laying out the wool base. It is important to stop at the edge of the form, because after wetting

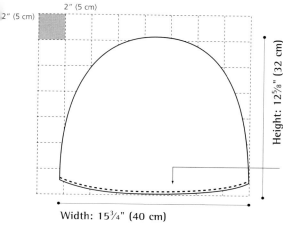

2" (5 cm)

2" (5 cm)

Height: 12⅝" (32 cm)

This beginner's pattern produces a 2" (5 cm) brim. With experience, it is possible to slightly increase the size and shape of the form, and shrink the felt a little more to produce the same hat but with a denser fabric.

Finished head size:
21¾" to 22½" (55 to 57 cm)

Width: 15¾" (40 cm)

the fibers will naturally relax and extend further from the edge. Wetted layers of fibers extending ¾" to 1" (2 to 2.5 cm) are appropriate for folding over. If the fibers extend more than that, the overlapping portion may become too thick. It is much easier to add to the extending wool if the layer is too thin, than to pull off extra wet wool.

5 |

Lay a plastic net over the base wool and sprinkle it generously with hot felting solution. With a plastic bag over your hand, gently rub the net so that the felting solution spreads through-out the wool, pressing out any air at the same time.

6 |

Remove the net, cover the form with another plastic sheet, and carefully flip it over. Remove the top plastic sheet.

7 |

Pull the extending wool base ends up and over the form. Do not overlap at the corners, but pull the fibers toward the center of the form, taking care to avoid any wrinkles and open spaces.

8 |

Repeat steps 4b through 6 for the remaining four sections.

9 |

Pull the protruding wool ends from the underside up and over the edges. Splay

the corner wrinkles by pulling gently toward the center of the form. Do not fold or overlap the ends at the corners.

10 |

For the remaining hat base color B:
Divide color B top into eight equal sections and repeat steps 4a through 9.

4b

5

6

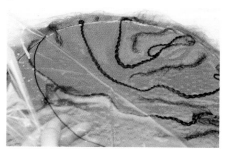

7

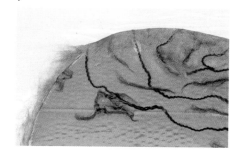

8

9

10

11

12

13a

13b

14

Flower Chapeau

Pink Dread Hat

11

Continue with all layers of color B, but reserve a little extra wool from one layer for reinforcing the crown of the hat. Lay out the extra wool diagonally on a small section on either side of the top or crown of the hat.

12

Wet and flip over hat. Fold over the extending wool while pulling on it gently. Hand rub it into place with a little felting solution. Finish laying on final four layers to this side, then wet, flip over, and fix extending edges.

13a

With plastic bags covering your hands, gently massage the hat form from the

15

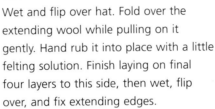

16

outer edges inward; avoid circular motions. Sprinkle the form with felting solution as needed. NOTE: Too much water or soap will hinder the felting process. Massage about fifteen minutes on each side. Don't forget the edge areas.

13b

When the outside layer of the base fibers appears stable, apply deeper pressure with your fingertips to work the inner design into the hat base. Work vigorously for five more minutes per side. The fibers should start to tighten up and feel like a skin around the cardboard form. Using a timer is helpful to keep exact track of the massaging time.

14

Do a pinch-test to check the condition of the felted fibers in several areas. Does the fabric pull up as a uniform skin, or are there areas where the layers pull up individually? If the latter is the case, felt a little longer on both sides.

15

Once the fibers have stiffened into a tight fabric, use your fingers to pull the bottom edge; this will straighten it and ensure a clean cut. Then, with sharp scissors, carefully cut off ¼" (6 mm) from the bottom edge. Make long, straight cuts.

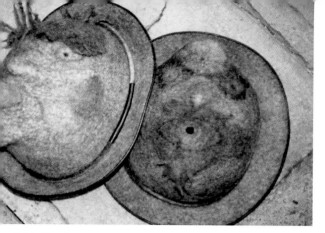

Whistling hats

18

16

Open up the hat to check the solidity of the motif. Gently work the inside of the hat, applying a little hot felting solution, until the motif elements appear successfully connected to the base wool. NOTE: Do not remove the form before reaching this stage.

17

Carefully remove the cardboard form and turn the hat inside out; massage the design gently. Once the design is stable, stretch and rub away any creases around the edges. Next, determine what kind of brim is needed. If it is to be rolled or folded, no stretching of the cut edge is required—skip to step 19. For other brims, continue with step 18.

18

For hats with straight or slightly rounded brims, stretch out the brim area by pulling horizontally along the entire cut edge, especially any areas that are thicker than the rest of the brim. NOTE: It is important to do this while the fabric is still soft and pliable, before it shrinks too much.

19

Turn the hat inside out again and place a thin plastic sheet inside.

20

Lay out, one on top of the other, a towel, a thin plastic sheet, the hat, and a medium-diameter rolling pipe. Roll up the hat and plastic sheet together

around the pipe, then tightly roll up the bundle in the towel to secure it.

21

Roll thirty counts (up and back equaling one count). Open up the bundle, and shift the edge fold position 2" (5 cm) to the right. Rotate the position of the hat, clockwise, on the plastic sheet, so that the rolling is widthwise. Roll with even pressure and with the same amount of rolls for each rotation. Shift the edge position between each rolling session, rotating 2" (5 cm) to the right, to ensure a final rounded crown form. Rolling in the same position each time will result in a fine "teapot cozy" instead of a nicely rounded hat shape.

22

Between rolling sessions, stretch the brim, and check and stretch the crown area or top of the hat, to achieve the desired shape. Pay attention to the hat's form now, because reshaping after the hardening stage is much harder for beginners.

19

20

21

17

22

A Lady's Hat

23

24

25a

25b

26

Trekking caps

Dessert toppings: Soft Ice Cream, Whipped Cream, Cherry Pie, Meringue, Coconuts

23 |
Using a short dowel ⅝" x 6" (1.5 x 15 cm) long, roll only the brim edge tightly into the hat opening, section by section, forty times each, to shrink it toward the crown. Repeat a total of two to three times, working both the outside and underside of the brim edge. This will strengthen the fabric in this area to achieve a stiffer brim. Stretch the brim to shape it after each rolling stint.

24 |
Repeat steps 21 and 22, four or five times, if necessary. Harden until the hat is slightly smaller than the size of the hat form you intend to use, close to 40 percent smaller than the cardboard form. (The hat form shown here is a handleless pan that is equivalent to an adult's head size.) Before moving to the hat form, stretch out the crown area first to maintain a rounded, flat-top shape. Next, slip the hat over the form while pulling at the base of the crown. Do not pull on the edge of the brim.

25a |
Use a short dowel to help stretch out a straight brim and smooth away any wrinkles on the surface of the crown. Now the hat is ready for the final hot water rinse. After washing it well, spin out any excess moisture, or wring the hat in a towel. Steam-heat the inside of the hat and reposition it on the form choosing the most becoming area as the front. Using a steam iron, short dowel,

and ruler, stretch the brim into a consistent width. To form a suitable curved brim shape, work the brim between your fingers and thumbs, as if making a ceramic bowl.

25b |
You can use a loop of padded cord to help create the slight curve of the brim. Fix any indentations in the brim edge by pulling with a pair of needlenose pliers or using your fingertips.

26 |
Continue to steam iron the hat until you are finished forming. Keep the hat on the form until it is dry; if you take it off too early it will probably shrink to a smaller size. For a decorative accent add a ribbon or a leather band (which also helps prevent the head size from becoming stretched out). Decorate to suit your taste or the occasion, such as adding a felt stick brooch or flower. NOTE: If you want a hat with a wider brim or a unique shape, use the template on page 63 as a reference to make a more challenging pattern. Add a wider brim to the cardboard form from the start or make an irregular pointed crown shape for a perfectly bent Halloween witch's hat.

MAKE A CHILD'S BERET for a special occasion, such as a piano recital or birthday party. Making one in a cute shape, like a heart, teddy bear, star, or fish can be a wonderful gift for any child. After making this flower beret for your daughter, enlarge the pattern and increase the amount of wool proportionately to make another one for you or a friend.

Little Lady's Flower Beret

Little Lady's Flower Beret

1

2a

2b

2c

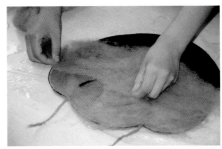

3

MATERIALS

- Template (page 69)
- Dyed fine merino 64s to 68s wool for base, total 1.9 oz. (55 g)
- Yarn for design outline and decoration, as needed
- Color-blend wool for contrast in petal and calyx design, in small amounts

1

Draw and cut out a flower beret using the template shown on page 69; tape the edges. Transfer the petal formation on both sides of the cardboard using a permanent marker. Prepare the base color wool for the petals (approximately ³/₄ oz. [20 g]) and for the calyx, or the area of the plant where the flower and stem join (approximately ¹/₂ oz. [15 g]). Use a slightly deeper shade for the outer petals (approximately ³/₄ oz. [20 g]). Divide each color of wool section into four equal parts.

2a

For the calyx: Place the cardboard form on a plastic sheet. Start by dipping a thin, lightly twisted, single-ply yarn of green wool in felting solution and laying it along the lines that divide the calyx and petal areas. Make sure there is enough of the yarn to go around to the back. Place four thin, alternating layers of the same color wool in the calyx area and wet it with felting solution to keep it in place. Trim any wool that is extending past the calyx area into the petals.

2b

Cover the form with a net and sprinkle it with felting solution to stabilize the design.

2c

Use a fork to adjust the edges and contour lines. Lay down a sheet of plastic and carefully flip over the form.

3

Fold over the extending green calyx contour yarn and overlap the ends. Gently pull any extending green wool over from the underside onto the top of the form. Repeat steps 2a through 2c for this side.

4

For the petals: Wet additional thin yarns of color-blended wool and lay them down along the contour lines of the petal pattern. Place fine multiple layers of petal wool on top of and just to the edges of the form and calyx. Lay a plastic net over the base wool and sprinkle generously with hot felting solution. With a plastic bag over your hand, gently rub the net so that the felting solution spreads throughout the wool, pressing out any air at the same time. Carefully turn the flower over. NOTE: If using batt, place two layers; if using top wool, place four layers if possible. To create a more three-dimensional effect, use darker shades of color-blended wool for the background petals and lighter shades for the front petals or vice versa.

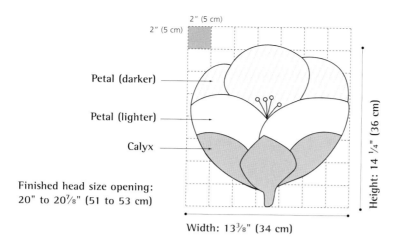

Petal (darker)

Petal (lighter)

Calyx

Finished head size opening:
20" to 20⅞" (51 to 53 cm)

2" (5 cm)
2" (5 cm)

Height: 14 ¼" (36 cm)

Width: 13⅜" (34 cm)

Neighborhood cuties

5

Continue to work the petal contour lines with yarn. Pull over the extending wool from the underside to pull the fibers toward the center and get rid of any wrinkles. Sprinkle with more felting solution, if needed. Lay out the remaining petal wool in alternating perpendicular layers, cover with a net, and sprinkle with felting solution. Remove the net. Cover the form with plastic and gently flip it over, then remove the top plastic and neatly pull the extending wool ends over the edges.

6

For the beret base layer: Lay four alternating layers of dyed tops (if using batt, add two layers) for the inner petals. Cover with a net and sprinkle thoroughly with felting solution. Smooth to eliminate wrinkles and air pockets. Remove the net and replace it with a plastic sheet, then flip the form over. Gently pull the underside wool ends out and fold them over onto the form.

7a

Repeat step 6 to lay down the remaining base layers.

7b

Mark the opening side of the beret with wool yarn, making an X.

8

Cover your hands with plastic bags and gently massage from the outside inward for approximately ten minutes per side. Gradually apply more fingertip pressure during the massage (about five to ten minutes more for each side). Confirm the felting condition with a pinch-test. If the layers have hardened enough that they are unified into one piece of fabric, proceed to step 9. If not, continue massaging until the hardening stage is complete.

7a

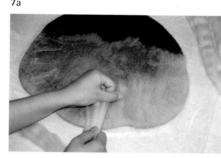

5

7b

6

8

9a

9b

9c

10a

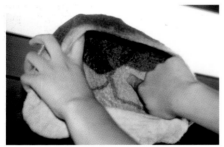

10b

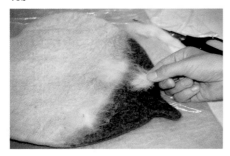

11a

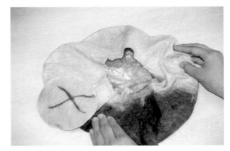

11b

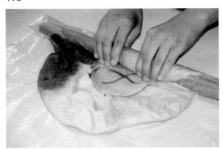

9a

Place an inverted saucer (approximately 5½" [14 cm] in diameter) in the exact center of the beret (covering the X). Using a craft knife, cut once around the edge of the saucer. Be careful not to cut through the soft, wet cardboard to the other side.

9b

Using sharp scissors, clip any remaining uncut fibers and remove the newly cut circle of felt. Gently rub around the cut edge of the beret and check to see if the inner wool fibers are well entangled before carefully removing the cardboard form. Try not to stretch the opening edge of the beret. Turn the beret right side out.

9c

Hand massage the surface of the beret to integrate the design layers further into the base, then work the edges to eliminate the fold lines. Sprinkle with felting solution as needed.

10a

Gently wring out any excess felting solution and hold the beret up toward the light. Check for thin areas where more wool may be required.

10b

To repair thin areas, cut the appropriate color wool into short lengths, blend it slightly within your fingertips, and apply a minimal amount to any area in need of extra wool. Sprinkle the area with felting solution and gently work it for a few minutes with a plastic bag over your fingertips.

11a

Turn the beret inside out again and insert a plastic bag so the design will not stick to other parts of the beret. Shift the outer fold line toward the center and gather the fabric up slightly around the opening to avoid stretching out the circle.

11b

Place the beret on a plastic sheet and roll them both, along with the cut-out circle, tightly around a small-diameter rolling pipe. To secure the bundle, roll it up again in a towel or a piece of cotton sheet. Begin rolling back and forth for thirty counts. Open up the bundle, change the direction of the beret, shift to new fold lines, and continue rolling for a total of six changed directional rotations of thirty counts each.

More fun berets to wear

11c

The finished beret should be more supple than stiff, so stop felting when the fibers are well entwined and the beret is about 15 to 20 percent smaller than the original form.

12a

Rinse the beret well in lukewarm water and spin or wring out excess moisture. Steam-iron while the beret is still damp to smooth the surface and make a perfect shape.

12b

Place the beret over the hat form and leave it to dry. NOTE: Sewing a ribbon around the opening during the finishing steps (steps 13b and 13c) adds thickness to the beret opening, making it smaller. If you plan to add a decorative ribbon, stretch the opening area larger than the final desired size or use a slightly larger hat form when drying.

13a

When the beret is dry, sew on a small bunch of yarn for the pistils of the flower.

13b

Cut and prepare two pieces of complementary-colored ribbon to be sewn over the edge of the opening as a decorative element. This edging will also hide the cut-edge and prevent the beret from stretching in size during use.

13c

Blind stitch the decorative ribbon around the opening on both the inside and outside. Be sure to check the opening size while stitching and avoid cinching the opening.

11c

13a

12a

13b

12b

13c

RAINBOW Jumper

IN THIS CHAPTER, we will incorporate the techniques learned in previous chapters to make a complicated three-dimensional standing sculpture, such as the Rainbow Jumper. After the felting work is finished, you will learn how to dye just the lower portion of the sculpture. If you'd like to, think up your own shifted shape make-believe creature, object, or toy. Almost any shape or form is possible, so have fun being creative.

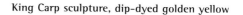

King Carp sculpture, dip-dyed golden yellow

MATERIALS
- Template (page 75)
- White 64s top for base, 1 oz. (30 g)
- Dyed wool, novelty yarns, prefelt, and silk organza bits
- Beads for decoration
- Polyester batting or old nylon stocking, for stuffing
- Mounting board or bubble wrap

1a

1b

2

3a

1a

For the decorative design layer: Cut out the resist form following the template shown on page 75 using either mounting board or bubble wrap. If using bubble wrap, baste two sheets close to the edges, bubble sides together. Place the resist form on a sheet of heavy plastic. Starting with the finer details, such as yarns, arrange the elements of the decorative motif on the form. Dip each bit in a bowl of felting solution before placing it on the form to keep from sliding out of place. In a few areas, position secondary-level motif items, such as organza, down, and carded colored wool (see page 110 for carding wool). Don't overdo it; leaving some areas of the base color free of design is nice and helps emphasize the sculpture's shape.

1b

Cover the shape with a net, apply felting solution to thoroughly wet the design, and press out any air pockets. Carefully remove the net, cover the shape with another plastic sheet, and gently turn it over. Remove the top sheet of plastic.

2

Pull up and over any design elements, such as wool or yarn extending from the underside, and place them on top of the form. Complete the decorative design on this side. When the motif is ready, repeat step 1b and turn it over. To complete the 360 degree design, tightly pull up and over any wool, fabric, or yarn extending from the underside.

3a

For the base layer: Divide the white tops into eight equal sections (four sections per side). Starting with two sections, place two alternating layers, in thin wispy clouds, over the design motif and just to the edge of the form. In narrow, small, or complex contour areas, cut the wool fibers into shorter lengths. Follow the wetting procedure as before to thoroughly wet the two layers, then cover the form with a plastic sheet and flip it over. Remove the top plastic sheet.

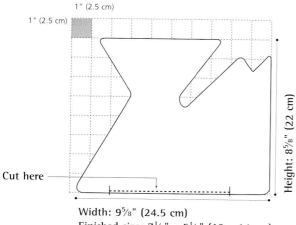

1" (2.5 cm)

1" (2.5 cm)

Cut here

Height: 8⅝" (22 cm)

Width: 9⅝" (24.5 cm)
Finished size: 7½" x 5½" (19 x 14 cm)

3b

Pull up and over any extending wool ends from the underside. Keep one hand covered in a plastic bag to help smooth down the layers without disturbing the design.

3c

If it is hard to fold over the wetted wool edges in certain tight areas, use scissor tips or fork tines to help.

4

Use two sections of white top on this side and repeat all of step 3. Check to make sure all edges are smooth and taut. Continue layering the remaining four sections, two on each side, following step 3. Make sure the white base covers up the entire design motif and the thickness is uniform over the form. Cut and lay out extra white top in any areas that feel too thin or where the motif elements show through.

5a

Once all the base layers have been applied and the form is thoroughly wetted with felting solution, cover both hands in plastic bags and begin gently massaging the form from the edges inward. Apply more pressure with your fingertips as the layers entangle into a uniform fabric.

5b

Massage the narrow and intricate contours of the shape, including the edges. Work five minutes per side for a total of about ten to fifteen minutes per side.

4

3b

3c

5a

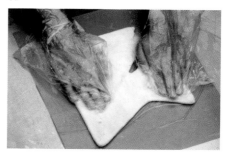

5b

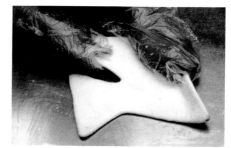

5c

6

7

8a

5c

As the wool shrinks and hardens, the pointed corners may become thin and the cardboard form can pierce through. Apply short wool fibers to those corners, wet them with hot felting solution, and massage that area for sixty to ninety seconds, making sure the newly added fibers adhere to the base layer. NOTE: Do not wait too long to do this.

6

Try a pinch-test to confirm that all the layers have joined into a single fabric. If they are not satisfactorily entangled, wet with warm felting solution and continue massaging. When the wool has formed a tight skin over the form, cut a slit in the middle of the bottom, leaving 2" (5 cm) at either end. Gently take out the cardboard form, turn the object inside out, and push out the corners of the piece using a blunt pointed object. Sprinkle the fabric with felting solution, and massage the design layer a bit more into the base wool, eliminating any wrinkles.

8b

7

Using a ¾" (2 cm) -diameter rod as a core, roll up the plastic with the sculpture; secure the bundle by rolling it up in a towel. Roll thirty counts, then open it up, flatten the form in a different way to get rid of any fold lines, and roll the piece for another thirty counts. Open up the bundle, sprinkle the piece with felting solution if needed, and repeat rolling. Change the direction of the flattened form for three to four more roll sessions (each roll session equals thirty counts.)

8a

Massage the narrow areas by hand. Push out the corners using the blunt device or pull them into place with needlenose pliers. NOTE: If you have any difficulty adhering bits or corners of areas, it is better to stitch or needle them in place between rolling sessions, rather than wait until you are done.

8b

The project is ready when it has shrunk 20 percent or so and the design elements are well embedded in the base fabric. Rinse it well, spin it dry or wring it in a towel, reshape it by ironing, and leave it to air dry. NOTE: If the finished piece is to be dyed, it should be dyed after a thorough rinsing, and while the felt is still wet. If you cannot dye the piece immediately, be sure to wet the piece well before starting (at least two hours or overnight).

9

Clamp resist–dip dyeing: The goal here is to dye red only the lower portion of the felted object. To safely dye a defined area, cut a pair of identical shapes from strong, yet thin, and straight, wooden (not laminated) boards. These boards, along with the fabric and the protective plastic sheeting, will be clamped together with C-clamps so tightly that the fabric in the clamped area will not be penetrated by the dye. NOTE: In order to prevent seepage, do not use warped wood, which will allow dye in to unwanted areas. To prevent any wood stain from marring the felt fabric, cut pieces of thick plastic the same size and shape as the boards and attach them to each inner side of the boards with double-sided tape. Alternatively, wrap the pair of wooden boards in plastic wrap.

Sandwich the damp object between the boards in the area you do not want the dye to penetrate. Tightly secure it in place with C-clamps, using a small clamp at each end and a larger clamp over the center of the felt object. It is important to be aware that rust from old clamps will also color the wool. Avoid this hazard by covering the steel portion of the clamps with plastic wrap, and make sure they do not touch any part of the felt object during the dyeing session.

10

Before dyeing, soak the clamped unit in warm water for ten to fifteen minutes. This allows the boards to soften so further tightening is possible. Next, safely suspend the clamped piece in a shallow dye pot before adding the dye bath. Here, sturdy dowels, longer than the pot opening, have been inserted through the open area of the large central C-clamp and are resting on the edge of the dye pot.

Prepare the dye solution following the package directions and follow all manufacturer's safety precautions. Carefully pour the diluted dye into the pot. Raise the bath by adding hot water; making sure that the highest level of the liquid stays below the height of the upper edge of the clamped boards. Continue dyeing as directed by the package instructions.

After the dye bath has cooled, remove the clamps and boards, rinse the piece well, spin or wring it inside a towel, reshape it by steam ironing, and let it air dry.

For finishing: Further embellish by machine stitching the mouth and a line between the front and back "legs." Add multiple beads for eyes, and hand stitch novelty yarn for a mane. Steam iron the piece and while it is still damp, and lightly stuff the head and body cavity with polyester batting or nylon stockings to maintain a good shape. Finally, sew the opening closed.

9

10

FABRIC
for Short Vests

IN THE HISTORY OF WOOLEN FABRICS, felt that is used for clothing
is generally boiled cloth, which before shrinking was either woven, knitted,
or crocheted. Aside from the ease of manufacturing lengths using these techniques,
the fabrics also tend to be more supple. It is harder to make by hand a wide
and sturdy piece of felt in the length needed for clothing.

This project makes a thin fabric with a uniform thickness that is suitable for a vest.
Unlike the projects made so far, the design motif laid down first will be the wrong side
of the vest; the design laid on top of that will be treated as the right side of the fabric.

MATERIALS
- 58s, or coarse merino, carded batts for base, 12.35 oz. (350 g)
- Dyed color-blended wool for design layer, 5.3 oz. (100 to 150 g)
- Decorative elements, such as novelty yarn (70 to 100 percent wool) and silk organza

1a

1a

For the base layer: Cover a worktable with a sheet of large plastic to make it waterproof. Lay a bamboo blind measuring approximately 36" x 67" (90 x 170 cm) on the table; compose a simple design with yarn directly on the blind. This will be the reverse side of the fabric.

2

For the decorative design layer: Arrange the next design layer as evenly as possible, using blended-color wool directly on top of the base layer. Supplement the design with yarns and pieces of silk organza, working the finest details last.

1b

1b

Thick batts can be divided carefully by pulling them apart to form two of the same length and half the thickness. Continue halving each batt until doing so becomes difficult and the batts start to shred. Divide these batts into six equal parts, and carefully place even thickness layers, in alternating directions, over the yarn design. Stretch them slightly during the layering process to avoid wrinkles later on. The layers should fill most of the blind, leaving 4" (10 cm) at the top and bottom edge and 2⅝" (6.5 cm) along the sides. NOTE: If the batt is too wide or too long, tear it between your fingers and weighted palm of your other hand after placing it in position on the mat.

3

Cover the whole design with a large net (such as door screening) and wet it completely with hot felting solution. Cover your hands with plastic bags, then flatten the layers and smooth out any air pockets. If necessary, lightly rub a bar of soap across the surface of the net to apply more lubricant for wetting the wool.

2

4

Gently remove the net, check for even wetness, and repair any areas where the design may have shifted. Smooth out wrinkles using the tines of a fork and your fingertips.

3

4

Opulent Camouflage Series:
Dip-dyed hat, inlaid motif vest,
and knit gloves with felt cuffs

5 |

Cover the surface with a thin plastic sheet, such as a painter's drop cloth, and press out the excess air. Roll the plastic, wool, and blind around a 2½" (6.5 cm) -diameter plastic pipe, 43¼" (110 cm) long and about as wide as the blind. Do not roll it up so tightly at first that wrinkles form. Roll the bamboo blind up in a cotton cloth and tie the ends to secure it for the rolling sessions. Tie either the blind itself or the whole bundle after rolling it up in the cloth.

6 |

Begin rolling by applying light pressure onto the bundle, using the weight of your upper body. After rolling 200 counts, open up the bundle, massage away any wrinkles, and fix any shifted design elements with a fork. Reroll the bundle from the opposite end, and roll another 200 counts. Turn the blind, wool, and plastic over and reverse-roll all together. NOTE: The goal is to roll the blind on the inside, with the plastic sheet on the outside. Don't worry—the blind will still give proper support to the wet wool. Repeat 200 counts per end and continue until the fabric length reaches 59" (150 cm).

7a |

Unroll the fabric and put the blind aside; smooth out any wrinkles in the fabric. With a helper, change to a 1¼" x 63" (3 x 160 cm) plastic pipe and tightly roll up the long side of the fabric, securing it in a sheet. Begin another series of 200 counts. Open the bundle, check for wrinkles, and stitch down any design elements that are not adhering well with polyester sewing machine thread. Pass some soap over the surface of the fabric, and reroll the long side, (from the opposite side), for another 200 counts.

7b |

Open up the bundle and check to see if the design is adhering; smooth out any wrinkles. Do a pinch-test to confirm that all layers have joined into a single fabric. Check that colored fibers from the base layer can be seen piercing and entangling with the upper design layer elements. Feel the fabric, checking for a solid inner core. If it feels "spongy" then further shrinking is required. Remember to reinforce the edges of the fabric by sprinkling it with felting solution and massaging the entire edge in short sections. With both hands inside plastic bags, pinch the edge between your thumb and fingers while rubbing back and forth. Work approximately forty counts per section. You may need to repeat this, between rolling sessions, another one or two times for the entire perimeter.

5

6

7a

7b

8

9

10

8

To facilitate the shrinking of the fabric, increase the wool's temperature by loosely folding it up and placing it in a steamer (ie., a deep stainless pot with a vegetable steamer). Using a minimal amount of water, fully steam heat the fabric for five minutes. After it is heated through to the center, quickly lay it flat on a large sheet of plastic bubble wrap, and roll up the short end for 100 counts. Open and reroll from the opposite end for another 100 counts; try to keep the heat in (the insular quality of the bubble wrap will help to retain the heat).

Between rolling sessions, two people can take hold of each end, rolling the long end of the fabric enough to grab, and then pull and flap it against the tabletop to stretch out the wrinkles lengthwise. Check for uniform thickness and how well the design layer has embedded into the base. (Felting is not always complete just by calculating a percentage of shrinkage.) Roll halfway to the center and work fifty counts; reverse direction and repeat. NOTE: The center of the fabric is the hardest area to reach as well as to felt.

9

Test the firmness of the fabric by pinching and shifting your fingers at the same time. (This is called a Handling Test, see page 132.) Measure to see if the fabric is 20 percent shorter in length from its original size. If it hasn't shrunk,

or the direction of individual fibers is still visible, continue to steam, apply hot felting solution and the soap bar directly to the surface of the design, and roll all sides until the fabric firms up. Rinse the felt in a large bucket with warm water while kneading it like bread dough. Continue rinsing, changing the water as necessary to completely remove any soap residue. Leave the felt for five minutes in a mild acid bath of vinegar and water (1 tablespoon [15 ml] per half bucket). Give it a final rinse, and machine spin-dry for two minutes. On a clean worktable, spread out the fabric and steam press the surface with an iron, using a heavy dowel to roll the surface flat. Straighten the edges with needlenose pliers and leave it to air dry.

10

Cut out the fabric following a favorite simple, vest pattern. Overlap the cut edges, stitch the pieces together, and finish with interesting buttons. Be careful to match the trim and buttons with the unique fabric you have completed.

Project results: A medium-weight felt fabric, $1/8$" to $1/4$" (3 to 6 mm) thick, $27^1/2$" (70 cm) wide, and 47" (120 cm) long. Approximately 17.64 oz. (450 to 500 g) of wool (base and color-blended) should felt into a fabric for one waist-length vest, with some fabric to spare.

MATERIALS

- Wool, three .5 oz. (15 g) portions, top or batt
- Polyester voile, three pieces 12" x 22" (30 x 55 cm)
- No. 30 cotton thread
- Long, thick needle
- Top-loading washing machine (or experiment with front-loading one)

The following three samples show the technical advantage of using a washing machine in the preliminary stages of felting (some people use a machine in the finishing stages as well, depending on the project).

This technique is used for stabilizing longer lengths of fabric, but note that it may not produce a desired final product. Some preparations are necessary, however, before the work goes into the washer. Sandwiching the wool between polyester voile and sewing it in a quilted-grid pattern helps trap the wool layers so they remain stable, and avoids lumping of the wool. After the washing machine technique is completed, the final hardening is done with conventional hand-rolling methods.

1

Lay the voile vertically in front of you. Draw an 8" x 8" (20 x 20 cm) square in the center of the bottom left hand portion using a permanent marker. Repeat for all three voile pieces. Divide one of the .5 oz. (15 g) portions of wool into four equal sections. Layer the four sections in alternating directions inside the drawn square.

2

Cover the wool with a net and wet it with felting solution. Cover your hands with plastic bags and flatten the wool. Remove the net.

3

Fold over the right portion of the voile, matching the corners. Baste the perimeter using a strong thread as shown. The stitching line should be $^3/_8$" (1 cm) on the inside of the wool square, thus trapping it and keeping it from sliding. Be sure to penetrate both layers of voile with the needle while stitching.

4

Using running stitches, sew horizontally, then vertically, across the voile, to create nine $2^3/_8$" (6 cm) quilted squares. Repeat the process for the remaining two samples.

1

2

3

4

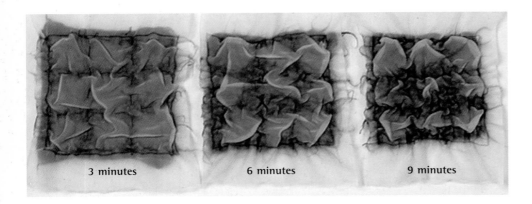

3 minutes   6 minutes   9 minutes

5

For the washing machine technique:
Depending on the washing machine
model, the amount of hot water needed
will differ. Too little water may cause the
agitator blades to rough up the samples,
but too much water will allow the
samples to float lazily on the surface.

Start by filling the machine with hot
water to about 10" (25 cm) and add
one tablespoon (15 ml) of washing
detergent. Place all three quilted samples
in the washing machine, along with two
or three tennis balls to increase the
agitation. Check the water level again
to determine if more is needed. Set
a timer for three minutes, and start
the normal wash cycle. Remove one
sample every three minutes (one after
three minutes, six minutes, and nine
minutes). The results are three progressive machine-felted samples. Rinse them
well, then spin or wring them in a towel
to remove excess moisture. Pull out the
basting thread, gently remove the voile
from the three-minute sample, and
reshape the sample with a steam iron.
Compare this machine-felted sample
with a hand-rolled sample of the same
wool breed. How are they different?

If the samples have agitated too long,
it will be difficult to separate the nylon
voile. The sample taken out after three
minutes has entangled enough and is
ready to be further hardened by hand.
The samples taken out after six and nine
minutes may be more difficult to
separate from the voile—if at all. When
using the washing machine, it is
important to periodically check the
hardened condition of the edge of the
felt fabric. Extend the running time of
the washing machine for projects that
are larger than the sample used here,
but note that 5 to 6 minutes may be
enough time. NOTE: It is better to check
more often, at shorter intervals, than to
leave something going in the machine
for an extended period of time.

THIS PROJECT MAKES a longer, semifitted vest out of felt fabric. It requires a longer piece of felt than the short vest, so instead of using a bamboo blind, the project starts with the washing machine agitation shown on pages 83 to 84. This technique uses nylon voile and thread to sandwich and stabilize the arranged motif and base wool materials. The vest fabric is then prehardened in a top-loading washer, and subsequently rolled by hand for further shrinkage. The edges of the fabric are not folded over so they will be thin and appear more interesting.

Elegant Long Vest

1

2

3a

3b

MATERIALS

- 58s to 60s (crossbred, coarse merino) wool for base, 10.5 to 12.5 oz. (300 to 350 g)
- Dyed wool for design layer, 3.5 to 5.5 oz. (100 to 150 g)
- Novelty yarn and silk organza for supplemental design motif
- Polyester voile, 36" x 90" (91.5 x 228.5 cm), two pieces
- No. 30 cotton thread
- Long, large-eyed needle

1

Refer to the washing machine samples (see pages 83 to 84) and practice this technique before proceeding. This will let you become familiar with the characteristics of the wool and its felting speed, as well as your washing machine, before jumping into this project.

Using the pattern on page 88, and the finished size as a base measurement, draft a pattern with a permanent marker by drawing it directly on the voile. Place four to five thin layers of base wool on top of the voile, inside of and reaching to the edges of the outline. Arrange an even layer of dyed wool design motif elements on top.

2

Cover the voile with screening, sprinkle it with warm water (no soap) to reduce the volume of wool, then press down on the wool to reduce it by about half its volume. Slowly remove the screen without disturbing the design. Fix any design areas that shift or wrinkle.

3a

Cover the wool with the other layer of voile.

3b

Cover your hands with plastic bags, then press out air pockets from the center outward.

4a

Staying ⅜" (1 cm) inside the wool area, baste the perimeter of the vest, catching both layers of voile in the stitch. Baste vertical and horizontal intersecting lines that create a grid pattern 4" to 6" (10 to 15 cm) square.

4b

Place more stitches in areas where needed to keep the yarn and organza design elements from shifting about during the washing machine agitation.

4a

4b

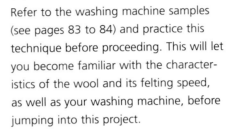

5

This long, wet length of wool must now be given a consistant hardness throughout the length. To help achieve this, fold in each end over itself, several times toward the center at 4" (10 cm) intervals, or along your stitching lines. Stabilize it by basting the edges and points across the folded portion so it will not unwind during the agitation process. This gives the center section, as well as the ends, a similar handicap for initial shrinking.

6

Fill the washing machine halfway with hot water and add one heaping tablespoon (15 ml) of soap powder. Place the bundle in the water. Throw in several tennis balls to increase the agitation. Agitate the bundle for three to five minutes (maximum). Check the edge of the felt, as well as the condition of the fibers passing through the voile. If the felt fabric is still too loose and the fibers have not entangled enough, run the machine a few minutes longer. Spin out some of the excess moisture for thirty seconds.

7

After spinning, lay the piece out on your work table and carefully remove the basting threads. Gently remove the voile from the felted wool without disturbing the motif, using one hand to hold the motif down and the other to gently detach the voile from the surface of the fabric.

8

Sprinkle the wool with hot felting solution, cover your hands with plastic bags, and rub the surface, working to join the base and the design layers and to smooth out the surface. Cover it with a thin sheet of plastic or painter's drop cloth plastic and press out the air.

9a

Roll up the plastic-covered felt lengthwise, secure it in three places with cotton ties, then roll it tightly in a cotton cloth. Roll for 200 counts, from finger tips to elbows, applying body weight from your shoulders. Open the felt, smooth out any wrinkles, and reroll from the opposite direction for another 200 counts. Repeat these opening and rerolling steps for a total of six lengthwise sessions, alternating starting ends, and rolling with the reverse side up for two sessions.

6

7

8

5

9a

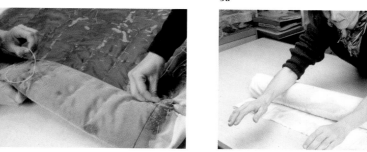

9b

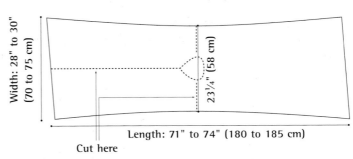

Width: 28" to 30" (70 to 75 cm)

23¹⁄₄" (58 cm)

Finished size:
24"x 50" to 52"
(60 x 125 to 130 cm)

Length: 71" to 74" (180 to 185 cm)

Cut here

10a

10b

9b

Sprinkle felting solution on the edges of the fabric and rub forty counts in short spans over the entire perimeter. The center area of the felt fabric will still be soft, so wind the fabric up to the half way mark and roll fifty to 100 counts. Unroll the fabric, then wind it to the center from the opposite end and roll again. Do a handling-test (see page 132) in several areas to monitor how well the felt has shrunk. To work the width, fold the felt in half or in thirds, and roll it widthwise for 100 counts from one side. Refold any sections just rolled to avoid making permanent creases and roll another 100 counts from the opposite edge. The width should be approxi-

mately 15 percent narrower and the length 30 percent shorter than the starting size.

10a

Rinse, spin, or wring the fabric in the same manner as the Short Vest (see page 82). Spread the fabric out on the table, and using a hot steam iron and wooden dowel, square up the shape and smooth the surface of the fabric.

10b

Pull and straighten the edges with your fingertips or needlenose pliers. Leave the fabric flat to air dry.

11

To finish the vest: Choose which end of the fabric is the better front and which would make a nicer back of the vest. Following the diagram above, cut the center-front line up to the neck opening; then cut out the neck area. Cut the shoulder lines toward the neck opening but not all the way through, overlapping 4" (10 cm) or so depending on your shoulder shape. Sew the fabric together again to form a slightly slanted and padded shoulder. Close the front and back pieces at the sides with buttons and leather loops or with bound leather button holes. Finish by sewing a knitted band or leather or suede strips over the exposed cut front edges.

11

THIS MUFFLER IS MADE using the simple, traditional technique of flat braiding. By substituting an unusual material, such as wool top, and combining modern aesthetics with a new form, this project becomes a unique variation of an old theme. I recommend using top with longer fibers and good elasticity, such as romney, which can more easily be separated into long strands. This project will also work with any merino or other felting wool you use often. Try using rainbow-dyed variegated wool.

Flat Braided Muffler

TOOLS

- Electric sanding machine with flat bottom and urethane pad (not rotary-type). (Do not use sand paper. It's important to create a softer feel for a muffler. Hand felting can achieve this, but a sander is a convenient tool for initiating the felting process and stabilizing the fibers, producing a faster prefelted stage.)
- Steam iron
- Spray bottle filled with hot water
- Cotton fabric; bucket of hot water
- Needlenose pliers

MATERIALS

- Romney (light gray) and dyed wool (romney, crossbred, merino), for pattern, in any color combination; 13 strands of 40" (1 m) lengths, 4.9 to 5.3 oz. (140 to 150 g)*

1

2

3a

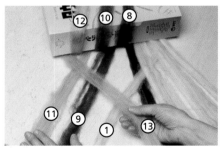

3b

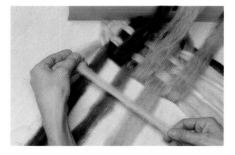

This project introduces a wool quality with a slower felting speed, but which can still be used for felting by employing a traditional flat braiding technique. The wool from the romney sheep comes in lovely natural colors and has very long fibers and good body. It also dyes well. It is known among hand-spinners as one of the easiest fibers to work with, making it well suited for mufflers as well as vests and blankets.

Wool top is handiest to use. In this case, the length of the wool strand is more important than the weight. In fact, you can keep adding on to the strands and braid as long a scarf as desired. Start with 40" (1 m) lengths of top, using approximately 4.5 oz. (120 g) of wool in total. The finished felted muffler measures approximately 7" x 67" (18 x 170 cm).

1

Braiding: Prepare 40" (1 m) strands of wool by subdividing the length of the top, widthwise, into three or four equal sections. Depending on the manufacturer, as well as the breed, continue to separate each section in half again to make eight or ten final strands. If they appear too thick, continue dividing but splay the individual strands into $1\frac{1}{8}$" to $1\frac{5}{8}$" (2.8 to 4 cm) widths. First, check each strand by feeling for even thickness down the entire length. If you find a place that seems fatter, gently pull out the area a few millimeters longer,

causing the number of fibers to decrease and making it consistent with the rest of the strand. Second, prep each individual braiding strand by carefully splaying or spreading out the fibers widthwise with your fingers so that it is possible to see the tabletop through the fibers. (Only after some experience will it be clear just how thin and wide each strand should be.) Try a short sample of 24" (60 cm) first to test the color sequences as well as the thinness of the final work.

2

On a smooth, snag-free tabletop, lay thirteen strands of prepared wool in your desired pattern. (The overall width is approximately $12\frac{5}{8}$" [32 cm]. Any remaining wool will be used later in steps 4 and 5 to add on to the length and supplement thinner areas.) Hold the strands in place with a wide, heavy item, such as a phonebook, placed over all the strands one-quarter of the way from the furthest end. NOTE: Start from the center area, as this makes working with long, delicate strands easier to handle. When the length gradually runs out, the braid is flipped over and braiding continues, adding more length as needed. Before braiding, number the strands (in your head) from right to left, 1 to 13. Start by lifting up strands 2, 4, and 6 on the right and lay strand 1 on top of 3, 5, and 7, ending in the center. Leave the strand in the center, to the left side of strand 7, do not take it all the way to the opposite edge. Return strands 2, 4, and 6 to their original positions.

3a

Lift up strands 12, 10, and 8 and lay strand 13 down over 11, 9, and crossing over 1, stopping in the middle. Return strands 12, 10, and 8 to their original positions. Lift up strands 3, 5, and 7 and lay strand 2 in place, crossing 13. Return strands 3, 5, and 7 to their original position. Lift strands 11, 9, and 7 and lay strand 12 in place, crossing over 2. Return strand 11, 9, and 7 to their original positions. NOTE: Tuck the edges of all the crosswise strands under the lifted strands so there will be good contact within the matrix.

3b

Make sure that the strand curves around at the edge and is not folded over, as it should lay flat. What's fascinating about this traditional technique is that each consecutive alternating lengthwise strand becomes the widthwise filler. This is a bias fabric because it is worked on the diagonal rather than perpendicularly. Continue braiding from alternate sides, always starting with the side with the most strands, checking to make sure the braiding structure is correct (follow the principle of "one strand over and next strand under"). During the first alternating thirteen strand moves, you should expect the muffler width to have tightened up to approximately 10"

(25 cm). NOTE: From this point on it is important to keep the width consistent, marking the new width on the spine of the phone book for constant reference while braiding.

4

When a strand becomes too short and needs an extension (or when a change in color is desired), prepare another strand as in step 1. Lay the end of the new strand approximately 2" (5 cm) on top of the shorter one and continue braiding. This is best done when a strand is about to round a corner and the weight of the lengthwise wool can keep the new strand in place. Allow the first half of the strand lengths to run out and finish one by one in a progressive manner. Braid towards the center, but stop one cross strand earlier each time so that the corner naturally squares itself off as you work. To continue working the remaining half, carefully flip over the muffler and turn the other loose end of the braid toward you. Catch up the braiding sequence, starting with the very center strands, cinching them while braiding to regulate the width of the muffler. Continue the "one strand over and next strand under" sequence.

5

As you near the end of the muffler, check the measurement; it should be approximately 10" x 90" (25 x 230 cm). If not, continue braiding by adding lengths to the work until the desired size is achieved. If there are thin areas at the end of the muffler, add in short sections of strands. To keep the braid from unraveling during fulling, baste and backstitch, 1½" (4 cm) from both ends, then trim off any extra fine ends of wool.

4

5

6

7

8

9

6 |

Since only two felting layers of crossed strands are used, make sure there are no gaps where the strands intersect. If there are gaps, splay the strands at the point of intersection to fill in spaces. A solid fabric will allow the fibers to entwine more easily. NOTE: On a lighter muffler you can leave holes on purpose, to make a lattice or lace effect, or even substitute ribbons, torn cotton, or silk fabric strips for up to half the strands. This substitution creates a totally different braided fabric with an interesting surface texture.

7 |

Prefelting with the aid of an electric sander: CAUTION: In general, sanders are not intended to be used with water. Keep the water to a minimum by steaming the fibers (do not use soapy felting solution; that is only used during the final hardening stage). Avoid being shocked by wearing rubber-soled shoes and paying strict attention to the amount of water near the machine.

Only apply steam from hot water during this initial electric sander phase. It is important to do the machine work while the fibers are moist and hot. Therefore, work only in 12" (30 cm) segments at one time.

8 |

Spray a hot water mist over a 12" (30 cm) area of the muffler until you see water beading up on the surface of the wool. Thoroughly wet a folded cotton cloth in very hot water, wring out the excess water, and lay it on top of this section of the muffler.

9 |

Using a steam iron (at the highest setting), steam-press each area the size of the iron for three seconds until you have heated the entire 12" (30 cm) segment..

When you have braided a long enough length, such as this muffler, you will see a pattern emerging. You can make a larger garment, such as a poncho vest, by making two wide or four narrow pieces, then shifting the design of one length to match that of the next to create a larger pattern. For a vest, blind stitch along the sides while in the first dry stages, reinforcing the seam by inserting a few short pieces of dry strand wool across the area to match the pattern. Be sure to leave openings for the arms, neck, and body before the hardening stage. It will look like a big potato sack but with continued felting the vest will become a seamless garment that has shrunk to fit. To make a baby blanket, prepare a narrower braid and continue to add on. Spiral it into an oval, then blind stitch it together using sewing machine thread. Felt it into a fabric as instructed above.

To make a collar for a jacket or an accent band for a leather hat, braid a narrower version of the above project, complete it, and attach it to the garment after it has dried.

Flat braid as a collar for a handwoven jacket (left);
combine two mufflers to make a vest (right).

10

Place the electric sander directly on top of the cotton cloth (or substitute polyester mesh fabric), for three seconds in each contiguous area covered by the sander base. First sand horizontally, then vertically, and finally, diagonally. Apply even pressure from the weight of your upper body to the entire moistened 12" (30 cm) area. You may decide to increase the sander time to five seconds after testing how your chosen fiber reacts. Gently remove the cloth. Repeat steps 8, 9, and 10 for each segment until the entire length of the muffler is completed. When the front side is finished, carefully turn over the muffler and repeat the same procedure for the back side.

11

Fulling (hardening): Remove the cotton sheet and roll the scarf up in a bundle. In a small basin filled with a small amount of warm felting solution, gently knead the bundle for thirty simultaneous squeeze and rolls to promote the further entangling of the fibers. Unwind and re-roll the scarf from the opposite end, then gently knead for another thirty squeeze and rolls. Repeat this process four times and wring out the extra moisture with a towel.

12

Using a 1" (2.5 cm) -diameter dowel as a core, roll up the muffler and secure the bundle in a cotton sheet. Roll for fifty counts twice, once from each end. Turn over the muffler and roll for another fifty counts from each end. Repeat several more times, squeezing out the cooled felting solution and applying hot felting solution in between rolling. To shrink the width, if needed, place a sheet of plastic over the center of the muffler and fold the fabric in thirds, then roll it widthwise for fifty counts to make it slightly narrower. Unroll, reposition the fold lines, and re-roll the scarf from the opposite side for fifty counts. Check to see if the muffler has shrunk to the desired size (10 percent smaller in width, 20 percent smaller in length). NOTE: This should be a soft material, not too stiff, but the fibers should be fulled enough so that jewelry items do not readily get caught in the scarf.

13

Wash the scarf in lukewarm water until all the soap is completely rinsed out, and soak it in a weak vinegar bath (half a bucket of cold water with one tablespoon [15 ml] cooking vinegar) for five minutes. Spin or wring out excess moisture in a towel; then steam iron the surface, straightening the edges by pulling with your fingertips or using a pair of needlenose pliers. Leave the scarf on a flat surface to dry.

10

11

12

13

THIS UNUSUAL PROJECT has a hidden structural support: a sheer viscose scarf sandwiched between layers of mohair novelty yarn. The result of this lamination-felting technique is an interesting pattern, as well as a very warm scarf with a nice drape. Using mohair yarn produces a beautiful sheen on the surface of the work.

Mohair Yarn Scarf

MATERIALS

- Mohair novelty yarn (80 to 100 percent wool blend with soft long fibers), approximately 1.76 oz. or 110 yd (50g; 100 m) skein per side; two skeins (or equivalent total amount in leftovers)
- Sheer or loosely woven rectangular scarf (cotton, rayon, silk, or 100 percent viscose), with finished edges, roughly measuring 14" x 75" (35 x 190 cm)
- Bubble wrap, 10" (4 cm) wider and longer than the fabric on all sides, two sheets

Although this looks like a simple project, it is a delicate procedure. When working with mohair, patience is needed to recognize when the fibers have successfully pierced the viscose scarf and entangled sufficiently to proceed to the scarf's final stage. I recommend that you tackle this project after you have acquired some experience in felting and have a general understanding of the degree of difficulty of this technique.

1

Lay a sheet of plastic bubble wrap bubble side down on a worktable. Place the scarf on top and wet it thoroughly with felting solution. Smooth out the scarf as large as it will stretch and make sure the fabric is wet; this will help the mohair yarn stick to the surface while you are laying it out. Start with one yarn, laying zigzag "squiggle" squares down in comfortable finger-width spans, in consecutive vertical and horizontal windows. Continue without cutting the yarn, or until you want to make a color change by tying on another yarn. Work the pattern until the scarf surface is covered (see diagram on page 96).

NOTE: It is important to arrange the yarn in evenly spaced and fairly dense patterns: about five threads per 2" (1 thread per cm). This way the limited number of fibers will entangle securely while also piercing the fabric and meshing with the fibers from the reverse side.

2a

Slowly cover the design with a long, pliable polyester mesh net and wet it with warm felting solution. Cover your hands with plastic bags, then briefly work the felting solution into the yarn and cloth using vertical and horizontal movements. Do not overwork the design, as this may cause the mohair fibers to pierce and get caught in the net.

2b

Slowly remove the net and reset any areas that may have shifted using your fingertips. Stretch out and evenly space the lines of yarn. Make sure the yarn design reaches the edges of the scarf.

3

Place the smooth side of a second piece of bubble wrap on top of the scarf and gently flip everything over. Remove the first sheet of bubble wrap.

1

2a

2b

3

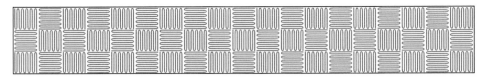

Width: 75" (190 cm)
Height: 14" (35 cm)
Finished size: 7" x 51" (18 x 130 cm)

4

5a

5b

6

4

The fabric becomes slightly transparent when wet, so the yarn pattern on the reverse side should be somewhat visible. Working in a reverse pattern (meaning that wherever yarn was vertically laid down on the underside, lay the new length of yarn horizontally), arrange the remaining skein until the surface is covered. Be sure to lay the wool right to the rolled edges. Upon completion, repeat step 2. After wetting thoroughly, and before removing the net, blot up any excess felting solution with a towel. NOTE: Too much felting solution will create a tsunami effect when rolling up the work and will flush the yarn out of place.

5a

Replace the upper sheet of bubble wrap, smooth side down. With a 1¼" (3 cm) -diameter rod, wind up the layers tightly while taking care not to create any wrinkles in the scarf. Check to prevent shifting of the design.

5b

Secure the bundle by rolling it in a cotton sheet, and tie it off with strings or secure it with rubber bands at either end. With minimum pressure, roll for 200 counts, then open up the bundle and roll from the opposite end for another 200 counts, checking yarn condition at edges only. Do not remove the plastic sheet yet, just unroll the bundle, flip the scarf over to the reverse side, and roll 300 counts from each end. In the initial stage of agitation it is important to coax the fibers through the fabric with gentle pressure, and this happens during long rolling sessions.

6

Remove the top bubble wrap, cover your hands with plastic bags, open the bundle, and remove any wrinkles and/or re-align any shifted design elements by smoothing them in place. Continue massaging the scarf with hot felting solution and plastic bags covering your hands. Use movements that follow the direction of the yarn layout. Turn over the work and repeat on the other side. Wind the scarf up lengthwise, with only one layer of bubble wrap on a rolling rod. Roll for 200 counts, unwind, turn it over, and roll from the opposite end for another 200 counts.

7 |

Spread out the scarf on the smooth side of the bubble wrap and sprinkle it with plenty of hot felting solution. Work the width of the scarf by rubbing vertically, back and forth, with your bare palms and a good amount of lather so the fabric will slip and slide back and forth. Gradually add pressure, but avoid wrinkling the fabric.

8 |

Do a pinch-test and handling test to confirm that the yarn and scarf have entangled into a single fabric. If not, continue rolling until the yarn has adhered. When nearly complete, roll up the scarf and knead it like bread dough. Throw it down on the table several times to help force the fibers through the fabric. Open and repeat the same

process from the other end until the scarf has shrunken nearly 40 to 50 percent from its original width and 30 percent in length.

9 |

Rinse well in lukewarm water, soak the scarf briefly in a light vinegar bath (half a bucket of cold water with one tablespoon [15 ml] cooking vinegar), and spin dry or wring it in a towel to rid excess moisture. Reshape and straighten the edges with a steam iron and needlenose pliers. Leave flat to air dry.

To finish the scarf: Check for any points where the yarn didn't pierce and entangle with the fabric. Secure any of these areas by hand stitching them in place so they won't get snagged by earrings or jewelry. If desired, decorate the edges with glass beads.

7

8

9

"Chalk Drawing" scarf series

"Chalk Drawing" mohair yarn detail

HOW ABOUT MAKING A PAIR OF WARM HOUSE SLIPPERS to help
your feet survive those cold, wintry days and nights? How about a design that matches
your favorite pajamas? An adult pair of slippers needs thick soles and sturdy fabric
to stand up to long use. This project will be a test of your felting prowess.

Warm Winter Slippers

MATERIALS

- Template (page 101)
- 58s crossbred, finnrace, or a perendale/merino blend, 6.35 oz. (180 g) total, divided as follows:
  pair of A side slipper tops (1.6 oz. [40 g])
  pair of B side slipper soles (1.8 oz. [50 g])
- Prefelt and yarn for design

1

1

Enlarge the template on page 101 as needed, which is equivalent to a young girl or ladies' small. Make a cardboard form for the right and left foot. Bind the form edges with clear tape (or prepare forms from bubble wrap). Mark side A (top of slipper) on both forms with a desired pattern. In this case, the decorative layer has navy stars with yellow yarn accents. The sole will be side B. Place the two forms on a sheet of heavy plastic.

NOTE: When sizing your own pattern, add a minimum of 1¼" to 1⅝" (3 to 4 cm) to the top of the toe and heel areas, and ¾" (2 cm) on each side of your foot. The more the felt shrinks and hardens, the more durable the end result. A total of 6.8 oz. (180 g) is used here but you may need to increase the amount to 9.5 oz. (270 g) for a size USA 8½ (European size 40), or more, depending on the size and style you need.

2

For the decorative design layer:

As with the hat and bag projects, these slippers will be designed, created, and then turned inside out. As such, the designs are prepared first. Begin by placing the decorative motif of prefelt and/or yarn on side A of both forms, with the desired side of the motif facing down on the form. Cover both forms with a net and wet them with felting solution. Cover your hands with plastic

bags, then lightly massage the felting solution into the prefelt design, helping it stick to the form. Remove the net, cover the forms with a plastic sheet, and gently turn them over.

3

Remove the upper plastic sheet. Pull any extending decorative motif from beneath the forms up and over, then wet them with felting solution. NOTE: Decorative design elements are not needed for the B side of the forms because leather or suede soles will be applied to the bottom of the slippers upon completion.

4a

For the base layer: Divide the two piles of 1.9 oz. (50 g) wool into eight sections each. Lay one section vertically, then another horizontally over the B side of the form, just to the edges. Repeat for the other B side. Cover both with a net and thoroughly wet them with felting solution to eliminate loft in the dry fibers. Repeat another two layers for both forms. Set the remaining four sections of B side wool aside.

4b

Cover the four layers of both forms with the net.

2

3

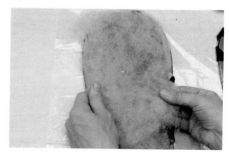

4a

4b

4c

5

6

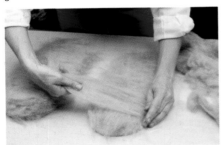

7

8

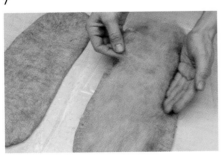

9

10

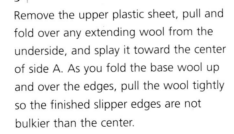

4c

Thoroughly wet all the layers with very hot felting solution and smooth out any air pockets. Remove the net, cover the forms with a plastic sheet, and gently turn over to side A.

5

Remove the upper plastic sheet, pull and fold over any extending wool from the underside, and splay it toward the center of side A. As you fold the base wool up and over the edges, pull the wool tightly so the finished slipper edges are not bulkier than the center.

6

Divide the two 1.4 oz. (40 g) piles of wool for side A into eight sections each. Repeat the same layering and wetting procedures as in step 4. Cover the forms with a plastic sheet and turn them back over to side B.

7

With the remaining four sections for side B, try to stay in the center of the form, as this will become the slipper sole. Place alternating layers and wet them with felting solution. Cover the forms with a plastic sheet and turn over to side A. Gently pull and fold over any extending edges. Layer the remaining sections for side A. Thoroughly wet the forms with felting solution, cover them with a plastic sheet, and turn them over again.

8

Tightly pull and fold over the extending edges, eliminating wrinkles by splaying the ends toward the center of side B. Place a small prefelt symbol on the heel to mark the "do-not-cut" side. Wet with felting solution.

9

Cover your hands with small plastic bags, then begin gently working the slippers from the edges in toward the center, moving in vertical and horizontal motions, and wetting with felting solution if necessary. Rub each B side of form for ten minutes, then turn them over and rub the A sides for ten minutes. Avoid massing the fibers at the sides of the forms. Repeat the process for ten minutes per side.

10

As the fibers and layers start to entangle and harden, apply more pressure with your fingertips while rubbing to work the innermost layer of design motif into the base wool. Massage using deep pressure for five more minutes per side for each form.

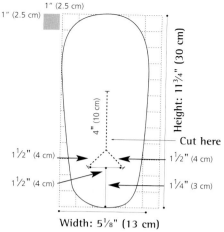

1" (2.5 cm)

1" (2.5 cm)

Height: 11¾" (30 cm)

4" (10 cm)

Cut here

1½" (4 cm)

1½" (4 cm)

1½" (4 cm)

1½" (4 cm)

1¼" (3 cm)

Width: 5⅛" (13 cm)

MAKING A CUSTOM PATTERN

Everyone has one foot that is slightly larger than the other, so trace the larger foot to make a pattern. Add a minimum of 1¼" to 1½" (3 to 4 cm) to both the toe and heel areas, plus ¾" (2 cm) on either side of the pattern. Remember greater shrinkage results in a stronger fabric, so you may need to practice with different sizes to achieve the desired result. Once you've mastered the beginner pattern, try working with an asymmetric pattern which more closely matches the true shape of your feet. Be sure to increase the amounts of wool as you enlarge the pattern.

Finished size: 24" x 50" to 52" (60 x 125 to 130 cm)
Finished slipper size: women's 6 to 7 (US)
Same pattern for left and right foot

11

Do a pinch-test by pulling on each side of the form to see if the layers have felted into a single piece of fabric. If the layers pull up individually, apply hot felting solution and continue rubbing each side briskly for an additional five minutes each.

12

Follow the cutting lines indicated on the diagram. With a utility knife and ruler, carefully cut an opening into the felt; avoid cutting through the damp cardboard form. Use sharp scissors, if needed, to clip through any remaining fibers. Carefully remove the forms.

13

Gently turn the slippers inside out. Sprinkle them with hot felting solution and massage the motif layer to make sure it has embedded into the base wool. With your thumb and forefinger, massage the circumference of the cut edge for forty counts in each area.

14a

Place both slippers lengthwise and with the heels toward you on a bamboo mat. Using a 1¼" (3 cm) -diameter rod as a core, wind up the mat and slippers and secure them with a towel. Roll for thirty counts.

14b

Unwind, refold the slippers to eliminate crease lines, then position both slippers with the toes facing you. Roll for thirty counts.

15a

To make very sturdy slippers, apply heat, soap, and strong pressure. Dunk the slippers in boiling water, remove them one at a time, apply a small amount of soap, and firmly roll each slipper around a dowel and in the mat and towel for thirty counts.

13

14a

11

14b

12

15a

These boots were dip-dyed for gradation and have stitched suede soles (top). The red slippers were clamp-resist dyed.

15b

16

17

18

15b

Repeat for the second slipper. Use the weight of your upper body to apply more pressure during the rolling sessions. Repeat steps 14 and 15 as needed to shrink the forms to size. Periodically check the opening size and feel of the slipper by trying it over your foot (covered in a plastic bag.)

16

To assure a proper fit, work by hand and massage the areas that may need additional shrinkage, such as the toes. Apply felting solution and roll the toe section for forty counts or until you achieve the desired shape.

17

Using a washboard with a slippery surface and shallow ripples, apply felting solution and further harden the sole, heels, and toes while shaping each slipper to the desired fit. The slippers may stretch with wear, but don't make them too small or they'll be difficult to slip into. Thoroughly rinse the slippers in warm water, spin dry or wring out any excess moisture in a towel, and reshape them using a steam iron. Place

This photo shows the difference between the prefelt, star-inlay motif (left) and the clean, un-dyed resist produced by clamping triangular-shaped wooden blocks on either side of the slipper opening (right).

a shoetree or crumpled newspaper inside the slippers to retain the shape; leave them to air dry.

18

To finish the slippers: Consider stitching leather or suede soles to the bottom of the slippers. Before sewing, cut a piece of felt slightly smaller than the suede and slip it between the slipper and the suede sole. This will give the slipper more cushioning and warmth. Make sure the edge of the suede and stitching line come slightly up the side of the slipper; this will prevent the thread that keeps the sole attached from weakening through wear. Alternatively, apply silicon rubber in patches to prevent slipping. To customize your footwear further, sew on felt beads, buttons, or bells, or consider embroidering select areas, needle-felting elements to accentuate the design, or stitching yarn around the opening of each slipper. You can also add an inner sole cut from a well felted fabric in another color for a contrasting accent. Dyeing the slippers after hardening may cause them to shrink further, so stop hardening the slippers when they are a bit larger than the desired size.

Now that you're more familiar with felting, I would like to introduce carpet making. Symmetric patterns are often found in the traditional carpets of Central Asia. This is due, in part, to a technique in which repetitive geometric prefelts, or thick, singleply yarn, are applied directly to the surface of large reed mats, or *chi*. The prefelts are followed by the base wool, which keeps the design in place. To begin this carpet project, prepare the base and design layers indoors where there is no wind to disturb your design. Then, when it is time to wet the carpet, take it outside. It's quite a job to do alone, so plan to invite some friends over (on a calm, slightly overcast day) to join the nomadic carpet-making party.

Colorful Carpets

TOOLS

- Cotton rope, ¼" (6 mm) diameter, 11 yd (10 m) long, for wrapping the bundle
- Nylon rope, such as the strong plastic rope used at construction sites, ⅜" (1 cm) diameter, 13 yd (12 m) long, for rolling the bundle
- Densely woven grass or plastic mat, 50" x 102" (127 x 260 cm), or available sizes stitched together
- Cotton work gloves
- PVC pipe, 2⅜" (6 cm) diameter, 39" (1 m) long
- PVC pipe, 1¼" (3 cm) diameter, 6½' (2 m) long
- Wooden rod, 1" (2.5 cm) diameter, 36" (1 m) long
- Brown wrapping paper

MATERIALS

- White wool for base, such as the South American crossbred used here (or other strong, slightly coarse wool, 54s to 58s, like Karakul, Mongolian Fattail, etc.), 2.2 lb to 2.65 lb (1 to 1.2 kg)
- Old cotton sheets (36" x 62" [91.5 x 157.5 cm]), two
- Dyed or natural color carded wool, single ply 100 percent wool yarn
- Thick, soft prefelt

Initial layout size: 36" x 62" (91.5 x 157.5 cm)
Finished size after hardening: 31" x 51" (78.5 x 129.5 cm)

1

2

3a

3b

1

For the decorative design layers:

Spread out a large sheet of thick plastic and place the mat on top. Wet the mat to make it more pliable. Use a permanent marker to draw the rectangular outline on the cotton sheet, followed by the design sketch, in thick lines. Stretch the sheet out over the wet mat and dampen it. Arrange the design elements directly on the sheet, with the desired side down.

Technique options for design:

I. Spin long, single-ply yarn from colored wool by drawing out short sections from the prepared wool top or hand-carded batts. Roll it under your palm and down your thigh several times. You can extend this wool yarn as needed by twisting on extra wool while laying down the carpet design, or use thick, loosely spun, 100 percent wool-knitting yarn.

II. Cut out geometric figures, letters, or other shapes from thick prefelt (because the carpet is thicker than the shoulder bag or the hat, the prefelt should also be slightly softer and thicker).

III. Make small, soft "puff" balls that will become dots when felted.

IV. Color-blend areas of the design with hand carders.

V. Prepare fringe or tails (see page 50) to be placed between the base layers after the design phase has been finished.

NOTE: During the shrinking and hardening phases, both the design elements and the areas surrounding the elements will decrease in size. As a result, incredibly detailed designs are not appropriate for rugs; instead, create large, clear designs with exaggerated spaces between the motifs for a true effect. I recommend using the technique that the traditional feltmakers of Central Asia use: Arrange the design bits starting from the center of the carpet and work outwards, adding the outer borders last.

2

When the basic design is in place, fill in the spaces between the design elements with the white base wool to achieve a uniform thickness throughout the layer. Complete the border areas at this stage by laying out an even thickness of colored wool around the entire carpet.

3a

For the base layer: Divide the base wool into equal amounts. The number of layers depends on the state and quality of the prepared wool. Here the wool has been carded into batts; these rather thick three batts, totaling the amount we need, have then been separated by layers of thickness and made into six, evenly thin layers. Lay the first thin layer of wool just to the line drawn on the cotton sheet, separating the excess area of the batt by carefully ripping it between your hands.

Rainbow Puddle carpet

Children's reading carpet

4a

4b

5

6

7

3b

Alternate the direction of the fiber for every layer, and stretch the batt as you lay it out to avoid wrinkles when wetting. Overlap and fray the seams slightly when working the width. This carpet uses wool in batt form, but layers of wool top may also be used.

4a

Don't forget to date and sign the carpet, if desired, on top of the last base layer, by "writing" the necessary information with the single-ply yarn or adding a simple mark cut from prefelt. Cover the entire work with a large net, and thoroughly wet it with hot felting solution. To speed the wetting process, use an old pan with nail holes in the bottom, or pour the hot felting solution slowly over a whisk broom to disperse the solution evenly across the wool.

4b

Slowly walk on the surface of the net, moving in tiny steps from the edges onward to spread the moisture through-out the carpet and squeeze out air in every direction. Add hot felting solution where needed. Your steps should neither disturb the design nor cause wrinkling. Stop walking on the surface when the wool is well matted and looks equally moistened. If you see any little mountains on the surface of the carpet, add more felting solution.

5

Remove the net, cover your hands with plastic bags, and work the surface by massaging vertically and horizontally in small, 6" (15 cm) squares. Stretch open, rub gently, and shrink away any large wrinkles while smoothing the surface of the back side of the carpet. Apply felting solution where it is still dry on the inside layers and work away any air pockets.

6

Fold the wool edges of the carpet onto itself; at the corners, remember to splay the edges to square them off, rather than fold them over each other. (Folding the corners makes them too thick.) Check for uniform thickness around the perimeter, adding a little wool inside the fold area at the edge if it appears too thin. To stabilize the edges, sprinkle them with felting solution and massage them. Another option is to trim the excess wool from the edges and leave them unturned.

7

Cover the carpet with another wet sheet; fold back any extending sheeting from the edge of the mat. Use the 2³⁄₈" (6 cm) PVC pipe to wind up the carpet, sheets, and mat. Lift up the bundle slightly with each turn to prevent wrinkles.

8a

8b

8c

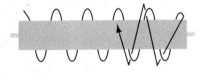

8d

9a

9b

10a

8a

Lay the cotton rope in an undulating zigzag pattern in front of the rolled mat. Start by making a knot in the middle of the cotton rope. Place the knot in the center in front of the rolled carpet. Starting from the center, make loops about 12″ (30 cm) long continuously up and down toward each edge.

8b

Roll the bundle onto the centerline of the loops. Working from each side toward the center, pass each free end of the rope through the loops, alternating front and back, like lacing shoes (follow the diagram in figure 8c).

8c

Meet the ends in the middle. Pull the rope through each loop again to really tighten it; tie both ends off well in the center. Try not to create creases in the mat by tightening too much, as this may also cause wrinkles in the carpet itself. It is important that the same amount of tightening is exerted throughout so that the size of the bundle remains the same.

8d

Twist and weave the bow and ends under the knot and through the loops, so they can't flap and come untied during the rolling session. Wrap a plastic rope once around the mat, crossing over itself in the center of the carpet bundle.

9a

For rolling: Have one person stand at each end of the rope, alternatively pulling and giving out rope to propel the bundle back and forth on a paved surface. Wear light work gloves to protect your hands. Roll smoothly and slowly while pulling (not jerking) on the rope. Continue rolling without stopping for fifteen minutes. Allow the bundle to turn around freely. NOTE: It is better to start with shorter rolling sessions at first and extend the time by five to ten minutes once you are confident the design is embedding into the base and that the base is not wrinkling.

9b

Open up the mat. Flip over the carpet and try to remove the top sheet, carefully checking that no design is sticking to it. If the wool is sticking to the sheet, do not remove it but instead wet the surface, flip it over again, stretch it out, and roll it up again. Each time the bundle is opened, check the carpet for wrinkles, and try to maintain the straight-edged rectangular shape. Cover your hands with plastic bags, then work out any wrinkles in rapid, short, back-and-forth movements. Apply hot felting solution and gently rub the surface. The wider the motion, the more likely wrinkles will appear, so work in smaller zones, allowing the surface to tighten up in that area, then move to the neighboring area. Prepare for another rolling

Marching Band carpet

session by winding the carpet from the opposite end, repeating steps 8; then roll for another twenty minutes. Try to roll the carpet tighter while stretching it as it rolls around the pipe.

10a

Turn over the carpet and slowly remove the cotton sheet. If any part of the design is too thin, cut up some of the same color fibers and lay them on the area. If the yarn design has not properly connected to the base by now, try basting it in place with needle and machine sewing thread. NOTE: Do not wait to do this later. In order for the design to become well inlaid it must be properly set in place from the start. Wet it with hot felting solution and swipe a bar of soap over the entire surface before hand massaging. As the wool forms a strong carpet it can be rolled without the sheet.

10b

Wind up the carpet once again, repeat steps 8, and roll for another thirty minutes. Open it up to check the design and shape and then wind it up from the other end, repeat steps 8, and roll for another thirty minutes. As the carpet becomes firmer, increase the rolling time; the danger of wrinkling is past.

11a

After the four rolling sessions are completed, stretch out the carpet by folding it on top of itself in thirds lengthwise, and tightly roll each end in your fists.

11b

Simultaneously raise the carpet and flap it against the mat. Repeat three times to stretch out and realign the base fibers.

12

Reroll the carpet (steps 8). Tie the ends of the plastic rope together into a large loop and double it to make it half as long. Slip the rope under the center of the carpet bundle. With one person slowly walking backwards and rolling the carpet by pulling on the rope, two or three people move forward while rhythmically stomping on top of the carpet. Chanting "right, left, right" will help synchronize the action. Step on the carpet with even pressure and work the whole bundle from the center to the ends for ten minutes. Make sure each stamp is applied directly to the top of the carpet with uniform pressure.

10b

11a

11b

12

13

14

15

16a

16b

13

For the hardening process: Roll the carpet widthwise, using a 1¼" x 6' (3 cm x 180 cm) PVC pipe as a core, and secure it by rolling it again in a sheet. Roll for 100 counts using the weight of three strong upper bodies. Unroll the carpet, wind it up from the other end of the carpet, and roll 100 counts more. Check the carpet to see if it feels stiff. Continue rolling until it is almost too difficult to unwind it from the pipe.

14

Move indoors to finish the carpet. Check that the design elements are entangling well with the base wool and that the shape is correct. With two people working side by side, roll up the carpet lengthwise around a wooden dowel (1" [2.5 cm] in diameter). As a general rule, felt softens after drying, so continue to roll the carpet until it has shrunk 15 to 20 percent in length from the original size. You must also roll the center carpet area by rolling it up just to the midpoint and working for fifty to 100 counts. Repeat the process from the opposite end. Keep working until you are certain you have a strong, tight, and very stiff fabric.

15

For washing and drying: Loosely wind up the carpet, tie it, and wash out the soap by rinsing it well with hot water. Leave the carpet to drain for several minutes. Open up the carpet and hang it over a rolling rod outside to drip. Shift it so a front and back corner are hanging at the lowest point, allowing the water to be drawn down along the edges to these two corners. Leave the carpet for one hour; squeeze out the excess water around the edges, and bring it inside. NOTE: It is best to start the final shaping procedure while the carpet is still damp.

16a

For finishing the carpet: Lay out brown wrapping paper on top of a plastic sheet. Place the damp carpet on top. Using a pair of needlenose pliers, pull on the edges of the carpet to straighten them while steaming with a hot iron. Beat the carpet with the palm of your hand or a wooden mallet about 12" (24 cm) away from the edge, you are straightening. This way you will not stretch and weaken the edge but instead straighten the carpet from the inner area.

16b

Apply a hot steam iron directly to the surface as you roll a heavy wooden rod over the surface. Leave the carpet to dry completely. Remember to flip it over occasionally to allow it to dry as quickly as possible.

Hand carders, wool samples, and a blank book for making notes.

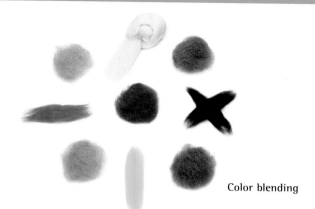

Color blending

ADVANTAGES OF CARDING

Having a pair of hand carders is essential for making samples of unusual fiber blends, as well as creating custom shades by mixing two or more colors. You can experiment with uncommon fibers, such as a pet's hair, mink fur, silk, holographic fibers, or bits of grasses, to create new blends with wool. (To achieve a firm, finished felt fabric, the combinations should be a maximum of 15 percent exotic material and 85 percent wool.) Color gradations by proportional blending make for stunning fabric bases, and new colors with added depth can be achieved just by taking a wild guess. Understanding the basic makeup of compound colors, experimenting with "marbling" of pastels, and testing for the perfect ground color blend will help develop your personal expression in feltmaking.

At times a felt palette may be lacking a shade of a necessary color. By blending the dyed wool by hand with either a little black or white, you can create the desired shade without going through the fuss and mess of dyeing. Blending is fun, like mixing paints, but instead of working with liquids, you are using fibers. You will almost always create an interesting effect.

Buying and Using Hand Carders

Hand carders come in pairs of paddles (made from wood or lightweight metal). They feature bent needles, or teeth, embedded in the surface of a leather or rubber fabric, which in turn is attached to the paddles. They are somewhat similar to a pet brush. Traditionally, hand spinners use the carders to align the direction of the fibers, making a wee "batt" and rolling them up in a similar style to the top we have been using, before spinning them into fine yarn. Additionally, hand carders are convenient for blending colored wool and mixing different materials and accents into fibers.

Be sure to select the carders most appropriate for use with wool. Consider the size and weight of the carders according to your arm strength and the size of your hands. Check for good balance, curved forms, and the right size pads, as well as an affordable price. While working with carders, wear jeans or an apron made of tightly woven fabric or leather to protect yourself from teeth scratches. These teeth are sharper than a cat's claws.

Drum Carders

The average hand carders are not made for handling much more than three to five grams of wool at a time. For larger carding and blending you'll need a tool called a drum carder, which can handle ten times the amount of a hand carder, or one to two ounces (28 g) of washed wool. This handy machine has two teeth-covered cylinders, referred to as drums, of differing sizes working against each other, and is operated either by hand or electricity. The larger drum surface provides a "batt" of wool, which is especially useful when working with children or preparing for larger projects.

Skillful Carding

The amount of washed fleece you are capable of carding at one time varies depending on the size of the surface area of the carders. Don't place too much wool on the pad at one time or else the teeth will not be able to catch each other. Use minimal amounts of wool and card quickly, rather than trying to work too much wool at one time. Place just enough fibers to thinly cover the pad area of the carder.

Move the carders lightly and slowly, as if drawing an arc, and allow the teeth points to touch lightly. Use a movement similar to lightly brushing your own hair. Practice will make this easier. Do not give yourself tennis elbow by carding too much for too long.

Five-step gradation

Carding Wool

1

2a

2b

2c

2d

2e

3a

3b

1

Always use washed, dried wool for carding. Select two colors of wool and start by mixing them briefly between your fingers. Place one carder on your left thigh, and with the palm of your left hand, stabilize the top part of the wool clump being loaded into the teeth bed with your right hand. Pressing lightly against the teeth, pull the wool straight out, while hooking a little of it at a time. Repeat the motion until the surface is covered, but stop when you can still feel the teeth under your palm.

2a

Place the loaded carder (teeth up) on the palm of your left hand, as if it were

a fiddle, with the handle facing away from you. Hold the other empty carder in the right hand (teeth down), close to where the handle joins the paddle. With a gentle combing motion, draw an arc lightly over the surface of the left hand carder, in your direction, trying to catch some of the fibers hooked onto the bottom area of the teeth bed.

2b

Transfer the fibers from the left pad to the right pad by repeating the motion.

2c

Do this several times until all the wool has transferred onto the right hand carder. Switch the carders and repeat the combing motion until all the wool has transferred from one side to the other.

2d

Repeat the combing motion until the two colors or fibers are mixed uniformly. This may take seven or eight times.

2e

If there is insufficient color tone, add more of the necessary color and continue blending. If you prefer marbled streaks, stop carding before the colors become completely blended.

3a

Gently lift the batt of fibers from the carder bed, with both hands, so as not to deform the shape.

3b

Slightly overlap and align the batts, like roof shingles, on newspaper for easy storage, or directly onto the felting equipment for a project.

Washing and Shearing Sheep
in the Country—from *Harper's Weekly*,
NY, July 18, 1868

WHY WASH FLEECE?

When using raw sheep's fleece, from your own sheep or from another source, it is better to wash out the dirt and fat (in the form of oil) as soon as possible. If the wool is not washed out, the fat will start to harden and eventually discolor the fibers. It is much more of a chore to wash the impurities out of an older fleece than a freshly sheared one. Remember, too, that moths are very attracted to a delicious, fatty fleece.

1

2

3

1 |

Start by pulling apart the greasy wool fibers with your hands and removing any undesirable waste.

2 |

Fill a large container with lukewarm water, allowing plenty of room for the wool to float, and gently place the picked-over, separated wool into the water. If the fleece is really full of dirt, repeat this step again. Washing small amounts at one time is more convenient than trying to wash larger quantities. Do not agitate or swirl the wool; instead, lightly press it below the surface of the warm bath.

3 |

To melt away the remaining natural lanolin oil, use a soap recommended for washing out oil and protein, such as dishwashing liquid. Alternatively, look for the soap used by hand spinners and designed specifically for washing fleece. Dissolve the soap in 122 °F (50 °C) hot water. Lift the wool gently into it, then leave the wool to soak for thirty to forty minutes. Occasionally, lightly agitate the bath liquid and push the wool into the soaping bath. If the wool is terribly dirty or greasy, repeat this hot soaping process several times until wool is nearly free of oil.

NOTE: Avoid washing large amounts of wool in too small of a container. Be careful when changing baths that the temperature does not drop too rapidly, which can cause a shock effect to the wool. This could cause the wool to turn into a felted fabric while you are washing it!

Mongolian lads and pals

4

5

6

4 |
Lower the temperature of the last bath to between 86 °F to 104 °F (30 °C to 40 °C) for rinsing away the soap. If the wool has released the oil and soap sufficiently, the washing procedure is over.

5 |
Place the wool in a laundry spinner for ten seconds (total!), or place the wet wool in a net bag, move it outdoors, and make large circular movements with your arms to whirl the excess water out of the wool.

6 |
To ready the slightly compacted wool for drying, gently pull it open. Leave it on top of screening or in a net bag so that air can circulate easily and dry the wool thoroughly.

STORAGE SUGGESTIONS
Store your wool in a naturally well-lit area with good air circulation. Place the washed wool in paper or muslin bags for storage; do not close the bag but leave it open to the air and light. You can also place moth repellent on top of the fleece, as its chemical components are such that their weighty vapor drops down through the wool. There are several alternative products to moth repellent with natural herbal scents, or try using a "smelly" bar of gift soap.

BREED/ COUNTRY OF ORIGIN	FIBER LENGTH (" /CM)	FIBER QUALITY COUNT (1 MICRON µ = 0.001MM UK BRADFORD COUNT (S)	COMMENTS
Merino (Aus, N.Z., S. Africa)	1³⁄₈" to 4³⁄₄" (3.8 to 12 cm)	17 to 23µ (100 to 60s)	Super fine, fine, medium, strong. Soft to the touch, high crimp count, highest felting capability, available in natural colors.
Polwarth (Aus.)	3" to 4¼" (7.5 to 11 cm)	21 to 28µ (64 to 56s)	Fine, medium. Soft touch akin to merino (Merino ³⁄₄ [ram] x Lincoln ¼ [ewe] available in natural colors).
Corriedale (Aus., N.Z., N & S. Am, S. Africa)	6" to 7⁷⁄₈" (15 to 20 cm)	27 to 33µ (58 to 50s)	Meat and wool producer. Medium. Soft, lustrous, available in natural colors. Lincoln or Leicester (ram) x Merino (ewe).
New Zealand Half Breed (N.Z.)	3" to 4¼" (7.5 to 11 cm)	27 to 31µ (58 to 52s)	Meat and primarily wool producer.
Crossbred (Aus., N.Z.)	2" to 4³⁄₄" (5 to 12 cm)	25 to 28µ (58 to 46s)	Fine, medium. Available in natural colors. Lincoln or Leicester (ram) /Merino (ram) x Leicester, romney, Lincoln (ewe).
Romney (N.Z., U.K.)	4" to 8⁷⁄₈" (10 to 22.5 cm)	30 to 36µ (50 to 40s)	Meat and wool producer. Relatively long, semi-lustrous fibers, similar character to Leicester. Due to the fiber length and thickness as well as elasticity, the resulting fabric is somewhat spongy and bulky.
Perendale (Aus., N.Z.)	4" to 6" (10 to 15 cm)	31 to 35µ (48 to 46s)	Meat and wool producer. Strong, lustrous fiber. If mixed with a finer, faster-felting wool the resulting fabric is of good quality for slippers. Cheviot (ram) x Romney (ewe).
Leicester (Aus., N.Z., U.K.)	7⁷⁄₈" to 9³⁄₄" (20 to 25 cm)	32 to 38µ (50 to 40s)	Meat and wool producer. Ram widely used for breeding. Long, coarse, curly fiber characteristics. Lustrous. Useful as decorative design element.
Lincoln (Aus., N.Z., U.K.)	8" to 15³⁄₄" (20 to 38 cm)	34 to 41µ (46 to 36s)	Animal used for breeding. Long fibers similar to Leicester. Very lustrous.
Cheviot (Aus., N.Z., U.K.)	3" to 5" (7.5 to 12.5 cm)	28 to 35µ (56 to 48's)	Meat and wool producer. Used for breeding. Very spongy, strong fiber. Semi-lustrous. Useful for homespun yarn.
Shropshire (N.Z., U.K.)	3¹⁄₈" to 6" (8 to 15 cm)	27 to 30µ (58 to 54s)	Meat producer. High quality, soft fiber. Useful for hand spinning.
Jacob (U.K., U.S.A.)	3" to 6" (7.5 to 15 cm)	28 to 38µ (56 to 44s)	Multi-colored fleece with wide variation within same flock. The white wool is softer than the brown fibers on the same animal. Useful for variegated homespun yarn.
Suffolk (N.Z., U.K., U.S.A.)	2" to 4" (5 to 10 cm)	28 to 33µ (58 to 50s)	Meat producer. A Down breed with spongy fibers similar to Cheviot. Used as batting fill for mattresses, cushions, and quilts. Not applicable for felting.

Wool is a general term used to refer to the fibers sheared off a sheep's body. Closer inspection will reveal differences in appearance of the fibers of some breeds. Wool fibers are actually classified into three categories: 1) "wool," or the down of the undercoat of the fleece; 2) the "guard hair," or the outercoat; and 3) the "kemp," which is least prevalent but is also found within the outercoat. When all three are present they grow in regular group patterns in the skin.

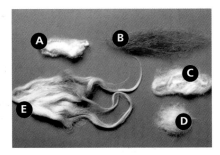

Wool clumps of five sheep breeds:
A. Merino B. Romney C. Cheviot
D. Down breed comforter filling
E. Drysdale

When choosing wool intended for feltmaking, it is important to know how to evaluate a fleece, which is the entire coat sheared off the animal, and to understand how different fibers behave under

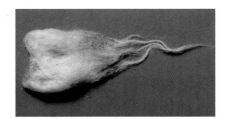

Long outer coat and soft inner coat (Navajo Churro)

different circumstances. Students should try to develop a comprehensive knowledge of wool, which will come about not only from reading literature but also by examining, sampling, and experiencing the magic of wool themselves.

WOOL FIBER GROWTH

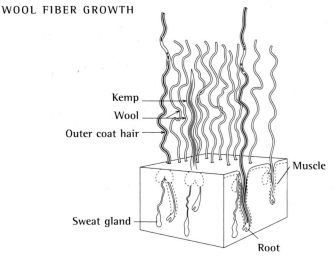

Kemp
Wool
Outer coat hair
Muscle
Sweat gland
Root

Adapted from M.L. Ryder, "Sheep & Man"

Wool is part of the skin of the animal in that it rises from the same cells that make the skin. This is the reason, coupled with careful breeding selection to produce finer filaments, that wool works so well next to our skin: It was created to be near skin. Let's study how a fiber starts its life and its purpose of protecting the sheep's body from the outside world, and thereby learn more about these amazing wool, hair, and kemp fibers.

FOLLICLES AND WOOL

Before two months of age an unborn lamb has no wool and the skin is quite smooth. Then small pits begin to appear in the skin. The bottoms of the pits begin to sink down to reach blood vessels for nourishment. The cell at the bottom of the pit begins to grow faster, rising up and pushing out of the skin. The bottom of this pit is where the root of the fiber is. The fiber is always growing the fastest here and always grows from the bottom upwards. This tells us about the fiber characteristics: for example, how the surface of the fiber becomes etched and creates the cuticle breaking away from the skin.

In actuality there are not as many pits in the skin, at first, as there are going to be fibers. The pits begin forming at the nose and grow outward. All fibers lean backwards toward the tail. Your pet cat is a good example to compare to as it probably adores being stroked from nose to tail but what happens if you stroke it in the opposite direction?

Pits, or follicles, need their own space, and for a while the skin is full with no room for any more pits to develop. As the unborn lamb grows, there is more surface area and each pit gets two supplementary smaller pits. As it grows another month the process continues and the pits develop more secondary pits. The bigger the pit the thicker and faster the hair will grow. Sheep, dogs, mink, mice, pigs, etc., share the same hair follicle growth pattern. If you have ever seen a pair of pigskin gloves you will be able to envision this clearly.

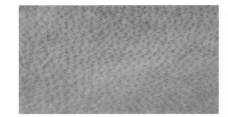

Pig skin

Under coat and kemp (Black Face breed, UK)

Crimp (from top):
Finnrace (Sweden), Corriedale
(N.Z.), Gotland (Sweden)

At about two months of age the guard hairs begin to grow, and on an adult sheep, these long fibers have the function like that of a straw roof on an old house, allowing the rain and snow to fall off the animal. These fibers are relatively straight, strong, coarse, and have at their center air-filled cells called medulla that actually resist moisture. The outercoat can also contain some kemp, which are also medullated shorter hairs. Whitish in color, the kemp helps spread or separate the fleece so it won't pack down. Because kemp lacks solid substance it tends to be brittle. In fleece from very high quality breeds, such as Merino, fibers with medulla are absent altogether.

Dense Corriedale coat

Later, at about four months, the undercoat or insulating layer of wool begins to grow, helping the animal to regulate its body temperature. As the cooler months of fall and winter approach, an insulating undercoat is beneficial for the strength of the animal.

This undercoat wool fiber is softer, has more crimp, or waviness, in its filament, and is finer than the outercoat, readily absorbing moisture. Selective breeding has reduced the predominance of hairy outercoats and has encouraged the growth of quality wool such as the Down breeds, which have well defined staples, or bunches of fibers that somewhat interlock during growth, or the Merino, which has very fine quality, lengthy wool with high yield.

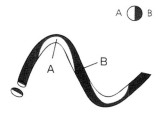

Wool fiber protein makeup
A= paracortex
B= orthocortex

Of course, there are some exceptions such as the long-wooled sheep Wensleydale, with its long Shirley Temple curls, or the Lincoln and Leicester which have exceedingly long hair-like primaries. The Hampshire Down, Suffolk, and Shropshire breeds

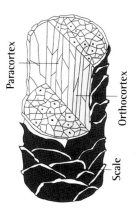

Wool filament structure

have skin with small pits and many back up secondary follicle pits (20:1)—smaller pits surrounding the larger pits developing as the animal's cubic surface increases during growth. The secondaries steal nourishment from the primaries, resulting in all the fibers looking like undercoat. The fiber length not only varies with the breed of sheep but can also have different appearances and quality at different locations on the sheep's body; the areas of the shoulders and back being better quality than the outer areas of the fleece.

One of the most interesting statistics about wool growth is the difference in follicle density among various breeds. Imagine, a fine Merino sheep may have an average of 36,800 to 56,100 follicles per square inch (2.5 cm); a Corriedale sheep 14,800 to 19,400, and a Cheviot breed about 9,420 follicles per square inch (2.5 cm).

CRIMP AND FELTING

One of the most important aspects of the fiber, as it relates to feltmaking, is its structure. For many years the theory about why wool felted was based upon wool fibers having varying degrees of crimp. Crimp is generally thought of as the natural waviness of the fiber, but instead of waviness, the fiber actually forms a coiled spiral. Because of this coiled structure, wool fibers can be stretched, and when released, return to their original, relaxed length. This elasticity means that the fibers have good recovery, and flexibility is an important factor in felting. The greater the crimp amplitude the larger the loops, and the greater the crimp frequency the closer the loops are together. This crimping is the result of the dual protein make-up, paracortex, and orthocortex of the wool filament structure.

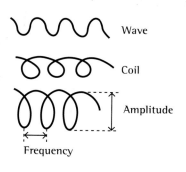

Crimp = Wave + Coil

In general, the smaller the loop size (and the higher the crimp frequency), the better the fiber felts. To prove this point, try making a sample of felt from two very different looking wools, like merino and romney.

SCALES, SERRATIONS, AND FELTING

After the discovery that the surface of each wool fiber has scale like patterns, the theory of feltmaking was revised. The scales are each fastened at the base of the core of the fiber and are free at the edges. The projecting edges of these scales form what are known as serrations, and the felting value of these serrations are largely determined by the number of serrations per square centimeter of fiber. Also, the general state of the edge of the serration, whether smooth-rimmed or saw-tooth, affects felting capability.

As a rule, the finer wool has a greater number of serrations than the coarser, and the more scales a fiber has, the better it will be for felting. A prized full-blooded Merino sheep may have as many as 1,200 serrations per centimeter while the wool from certain mixed breeds is coarser and has as few as 20 per centimeter.

So where did these scales come from? They were etched during the separation of skin and fiber growth, with the dissolved edge being left to the fiber. As the fiber continues to extend past the surface, the skin detaches itself and pulls back into the blood. Because the scales overlap as they grow up and out from the skin, they help prevent foreign matter from working its way into the fleece. The natural lanolin grease present on the fibers and the shinglelike formation of the scales work together to ensure that any rainwater or melted snow easily glides off the animal.

Scales are an essential factor to the felting process and are only present in animal fibers. Wool from sheep felts very easily by hand unlike other fibers

Cross-section of felt fabric magnified 100 times

such as rabbit and beaver, which need coaxing by industrial strength chemical solutions to assist in opening the scales of those fibers. Vegetable and synthetic fibers will, in some cases, intertwine but they will not felt by themselves. They can be added as decoration or filler, in projects where the wool fibers entangle around each other and around these non-animal fibers to hold them in place, but these "alien" fibers do not add anything more than mass and design.

Of note in this discussion is an industrial wool product that has entered the market called "Super Wash." This begins as 100 percent wool fiber except that it gets treated with chemical solutions that remove the scales, and a coating of silicone-based polymer envelops the individual fibers, making the fibers completely smooth and matching their look to something of a plastic straw. This modern development allows for 100 percent

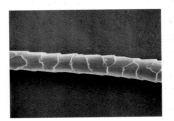

Merino filament magnified 1,000 times

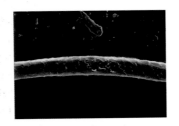

Suffolk filament (Down breed) magnified 450 times

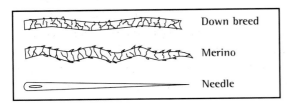

Down breed

Merino

Needle

ANATOMY OF SOME FIBERS:

A coarser Down breed fiber has a blunt tip and sporadic scale patterning; therefore, it is difficult to felt well. The merino fiber is wider at the root end and narrows toward the tip. The surface patterning is rhythmical with abundant, well-formed scales. merino has a slim, sewing-needle contour which gives good results and ease in felting.

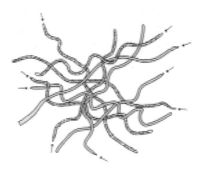

Under agitation, the wool fiber migrates from tip toward root

knitted wool garments to be machine-washed with no visible signs of shrinkage! However, if you try to hand felt this treated wool, even after thirty minutes of rolling, the fibers are still completely separate, like a plate of spaghetti. It is to our advantage as hand felters that the scales of the wool staple swell and expand under changes in atmospheric circumstances, such as the application of increased humidity, heat, shift in pH condition, agitation, and so on. Therefore, stay away from Super Wash products with coated fibers.

The shape of the fiber also affects its felting ability. A primitive breed of sheep such as the Scandinavian Gute from Sweden, a country with a history of felting since the Viking Age, has three types of primary fibers. There are more fibers at the base of the skin than at the tips. The outercoat grows longer than the undercoat and all fibers are pointed like sewing needles. Here we also may find kemp within the outercoat. The kemp fiber has a central, porous channel filled with air; it helps regulate temperature by letting air in and out of the fleece, but it lacks solid substance, which accounts for the weakness of the fiber. Also, kemp does not take color when dyed. Kemp floats through the felted fabric, making it easy for removal after the work is finished, or it may shed on its own during use. It may give a special effect to a yarn such as a tweed, but all in all breeders work at eliminating this impurity to make processing, removal, and dyeing less costly.

The fibers of the wiry Down breeds have uneven scales that look like dried mud and have blunt tips. The result in felting is that it is next to impossible to get these fibers to glide past each other to begin the entangling process. They tend to bounce back like a sponge. On the other hand, a finer, softer breed such as merino, with its even scales, pointed tip, and resilient but not stiff character, can easily find its way past other fibers and start to entangle and shrink into a compact fabric.

The direction of the scales, as explained above, means that the scales overlap toward the root of each fiber, and therefore, the direction of growth pattern affects the movement of the fiber during the pressure and agitation of felting. A wool fiber moves farther when pressure is applied from tip to root. This friction pushes the shaft toward the root end. If the fiber is free, then it migrates in one direction, but if the fiber is held down by

another, neighboring fiber, then that first fiber will bend and entangle under the friction. The entangling of the fiber reduces the distance between the tip and the root. When this happens to a mass of fibers in a fabric, it is recognized as shrinkage.

Fiber thickness is a key factor in the quality of a felt product. Thicker, less stretchy wool is suitable for carpets, tapestries, and perhaps large carryall bags, whereas softer, more flexible wool feels nicer next to the skin and therefore can be used for shawls and berets. In traditional carpet making, the longer wool of the first shearing of spring is used for the base and the shorter, softer, and cleaner second-shearing in the early autumn is laid on top.

The layers of thicker wool have more spaces between the fibers than the layers of finer wool, and the combination of the two fibers mixed together makes a dense, tough fabric. In addition, coarse fibers have large, flat scales while finer fibers have a much smaller scale structure. The size of the scales is also linked to the crimp. In general, the more crimp that is present, the smaller the scales, and the finer the wool.

FELTING AND THE DIRECTION OF THE FIBER

One key step prior to felting is the carding, or carefully separation of the clumps of fibers. After carding, the wool is laid down perpendicularly in multiple layers to form a base of even thickness. This cross-layering places the tip-root orientation in different directions and allows the fibers to move quickly and to fully entangle during the shrinking process. Actually, only a portion of the fibers are moving at any one time around those that are not affected by the direction of the applied friction. Therefore, it is necessary to change the direction in which you apply pressure, either by hand massage, rolling, throwing, machine assistance, and so on. During a felting project, vary the techniques so that each fiber gets a chance to migrate and entangle into the mass as you maintain control of the shape of the work. In the early stages of shrinking, there is more space between the fibers and the initial agitation allows for a rapid decrease in size. As the space between the fibers decreases, it becomes more and more difficult to achieve a higher percentage of shrinkage and to stretch the work into another shape.

Sheep Breed Samples

To understand the characteristics of different wools, such as its shrinkage capability and final suppleness of fabric, samples should be made under the same controlled conditions (i.e. duration of rolling, exact weight, equal pressure and agitation, and pH of felting solution). (See the Washing Machine Samples, page 83.) The tools and materials used, such as the surface of your bamboo mat (or bubble wrap or plastic sheet), the prepared condition of the wool (washed or unwashed, carded or uncarded), as well as the strength of the feltmaker, will affect the final outcome of the sample. Bear in mind, though, that there is no such thing as a perfect sample.

Before venturing out with unfamiliar wool and a large project, invest some time in making preliminary samples. These samples will prove invaluable in understanding the chosen wool and whether it will suit the project in mind.

MERINO 64s (SCOURED)

Fine, with good crimp count, high shrinking capability

MERINO 64s (Greasy/unscoured)

Felting process is delayed due to the greasy fiber. Also, it is hard to judge the true weight of the wool in the sample due to the presence of fat.

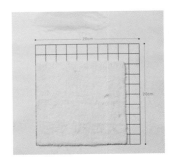

CROSSBRED 58s

As the quality count number decreases, so does the flexibility of the fiber; thus there is also a decline in the felting capability.

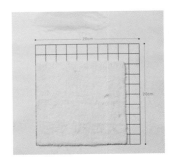

FINNSHEEP

A traditional breed from Finland, also called Finnish Landrace, now found around Scandinavia. The fiber is rather soft, rather fine, strong, and shrinks easily into a dense yet shapeable fabric.

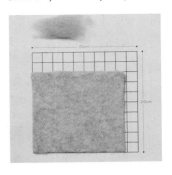

MONGOLIAN FAT TAIL SHEEP

A traditional breed of Central Asian sheep with coarse wool and a clear characteristic of a fat tail. Although it has a medium rate of shrinkage, the fibers entangle quickly and become a strong matrix.

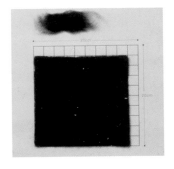

GREAT PYRENEES DOG

A sample made from the combed undercoat. To make a denser fabric it is possible to blend the slower felting fur with sheep wool for a higher shrinking rate (see owner's 15 percent dog/85 percent merino beret in photo).

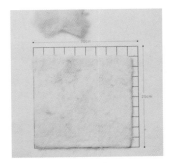

"Prize Merinos, 1845" USA

ROMNEY

Long, wavy, spongy fibers good for hand spinning. Shrinks rather well, but the finished surface is less compact as compared with merino.

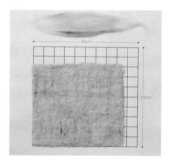

CORRIEDALE

Merino cross with Lincoln or Leicester breeds. Medium shrinking range but now tends to cater to the feltmakers' market.

PERENDALE

Cheviot and Romney cross. Within the crossbreeds this animal has a resilient and lustrous fiber. Can be blended with merino for strong boots.

ALPACA

Although it is expensive, Alpaca is available in beautiful natural colors and has a soft feel but poorer felting range. Useful as motif elements and blends.

DOWN BREED (SUFFOLK, ET AL)

Short wool for woven and knitted yarns. Felt has a loose, spongy quality. Entangles only slightly better than Super Wash processed fibers.

SUPER WASH

Machine washable, non-shrinking, factory processed 100 percent wool fiber. Final coating application prevents entanglement and felting.

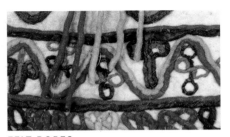

FELT ROPES
(UZBEKISTAN—HORSE COVER)

Lengths of hand-felted cords, dyed in vivid colors, establish the design of this decorative horse blanket. Coarse wool was used for both the fringe and cords, which were hand sewn to the natural white felt base.

MOSAIC PATCHWORK
(KAZAKHSTAN—"SHIRMAK" CARPET)

Two pieces of well-hardened felt of different colors are prepared; the design is then cut simultaneously through both layers. The design elements are switched, fitted back together like a puzzle, and then sewn together. For reinforcement, two cords (Z- and S-twist) are sewn in place next to each other, covering the seams. The couching technique is used to stabilize the surface of the carpet and to join the upper design layer with the under felt(s) to produce a very thick carpet.

APPLIQUÉ
(HUNGARY—TABLE CENTER)

Industrial white felt is laid on top of a red felt, and then, following the design of a stenciled pattern, stitched on the reverse side by machine. The white felt is subsequently cut away between the stitching lines exposing the red layer underneath. Abstract floral designs are commonly used along the handsome borders of the Hungarian "szür" herder's mantles made by employing the same technique.

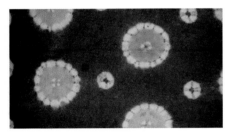

TIE-DYEING (CHINA—RUG)

When tie-dye techniques (specific folding arrangement and binding of fabric then over-dyed in two to three colors) are applied to felt cloth of moderate thickness and density, cross like designs can be produced. Thin carpets of this type, called Mongolian tie-dye, were imported to Japan at the end of the Edo Period (mid-1800's) and were used as tatami floor coverings.

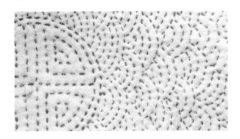

QUILTING (MONGOLIA—TORGUT
TRIBE; BAG FOR CARRYING A
BRICK OF TEA)

The stunning white-on-white traditional technique of quilting is often found on rugs, carpets, and yurt tent door covers. Stitching helps stabilize a weak felt fabric, and joins two or more layers together, producing thicker, thus warmer felts, and a handsome design at the same time. Here, a strong thread made of spun camel hair is used.

PREFELT INLAY
(CHINA—SHŌSŌ-IN CARPET)

Prefelt was used as inlay to produce the clearly defined, repetitive leaf-and-branch forms. Single ply yarn, as well a thinly cut prefelt, were used to further define the outline of the bird, its wings, and long tail. The meticulous attention to detail in this eighth century carpet expresses a felt pattern in color gradations similar to brush strokes.

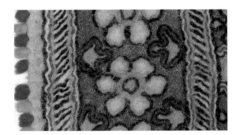

SINGLES YARN INLAY (WESTERN
INDIA—DOOR DECORATION)

Slightly twisted, colored single ply yarn is used for outlining designs, such as flower petals, as well as the striped border. The inner design areas are filled with carded dyed wool, and then all design layers, backed with natural white wool, are laminated together through fulling. The fringe puffs were sewn on afterwards.

STANDING EDGE (IRAN—CARPET)

The zigzag border motif of this carpet actually stands up from the base wool to produce an exceptional surface design. Thick prefelt bands whose sharp edges are cut upon completion of the carpet. Inlay single ply yarn and dyed wool are also incorporated.

EMBROIDERY (UZBEKISTAN—
FLOOR COVERING)

The entire surface motif of this deep crimson felt carpet is hand embroidered, leaving little of the base felt to be seen. Several types of embroidery techniques are incorporated here.

LATTICE (SAMPLE)

Narrow strands of wool top are loosely set up in a lattice pattern, piercing and intersecting each other freely, and then felted together. This system can be easily enlarged producing organic shapes or be worked progressively to form a more systematic pattern.

INLAY WITH NON-WOOLEN MATERIALS (SHORT VEST)

Use various novelty yarns, silk threads, and airy fabrics such as silk organza, georgette, or Indian gauze as unusual embellishment on the wool base before felting. This allows for the supplemental material to become embedded during the felting process. Machine stitching or hand embroidery will further enhance the felt surface after completion.

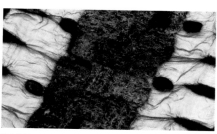

LAMINATION (EVENING SHAWL)

Mohair yarn of highest content is worked into an airy silk organza. The fabric and yarn are gently felted together creating wonderful textures and interesting wrinkles. Cut-edges can be finished nicely by laying and felting wool fiber on both sides of the fabric.

DREADLOCK OR TAIL (SAMPLE)

Direct application of wool top where the "roots" of the dreadlock or tail entangles with the base wool during the shrinking process. It is a suitable detail for carpet edges, unusual hats, or can be worked into loops for bag closures.

REVERSIBLE MODERN DAY MOSAIC (BLANKET)

This technique is made by simultaneously cutting design elements from two different color prefelts. Interchange the elements and stretch them slightly creating spaces between them. Laminate the prefelts together by placing a colorful middle layer of carded wool between them. Proceed with the shrinking process to successfully felt all three layers into one fabric.

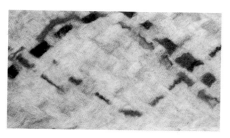

BRAIDING (MUFFLER)

The traditional technique of flat braiding is universal. Here a bias fabric is braided with lengths of thin top replacing the common cotton or wool yarn. Each lengthwise strand becomes the next consecutive filler of the wide braid and can be extended indefinitely by adding on more lengths.

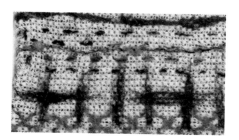

RECYCLED WOOLEN GARMENTS (SAMPLE)

Shrinking woolens, by boiling, or fulling, will produce a dense fabric, similar to a traditional Austrian Tyrolean jacket fabric. Here, loosely woven woolens are embellished with dyed wool top and yarn (either laid on top or roughly stitched through the fabric), then further hardened. Delicate designs may be needled into the fabric before shrinking.

CUT AND REVERSE (VEST FABRIC)

Make a felt fabric with different color patterns on each side. After drying, cut out symmetrical figures and flip them over in place. Stabilize the pieces by using a decorative hand stitch or machine zigzag, then steam iron to finish.

BRANDING/BURNING (MONGOLIA— MODERN TAPESTRY)

Designs may be burnt into the surface of a dense felt with a soldering iron. CAUTION: A soldering iron should be used only by an experienced person and in a good ventilated area, preferably outdoors.

The history of feltmaking is being debated more and more as archeological digs continue to unearth older objects. Up until recently, the primary scientific interest lay in the woven, embroidered, and highly embellished textiles rather than in the unstructured, matted, animal fiber, felt finds. This was partly due to the fact that felted fabric, although tougher than woven fabric when first completed, tends to break down more quickly under poor conditions. Reinforced, twisted threads of intricate woven materials last longer in such conditions. Luckily, the oldest and most exquisite objects to date were scrupulously secured in aboveground storehouses under nearly perfect conditions of conservation, or frozen in a grave of permafrost sealed off from air, for us to learn from and marvel at.

FELT LEGENDS

What the exact origin of feltmaking is and who discovered its ingenious and practical uses is difficult to say. Historians have known felt was used long before it was discussed in the first written histories. More recent history offers two entertaining legends about its possible accidental discovery, which are described below.

The first story is said to have taken place in the Middle Ages. One day, a French monk went off on a long journey wearing new sandals that soon began to irritate his feet. As he walked, he started to pick up pieces of fleece caught on rocks and twigs and perhaps even plucked wool from nearby sheep, and tucked it into his footwear. After some days, on arrival at his destination, he discovered the fluffy wool had matted into a strong, tough, useful, and comfortable fabric. Every year since that time, on November 23, Europeans celebrate St. Clement's Day, honoring him as the patron saint of hatters. A similar story about a Middle Eastern camel herder who placed soft camel's hair into his sandals for the same relief and comfort has also been handed down.

Another tale of interest in the felting circles is a special version of the biblical story of Noah's Ark. When Noah heard of the prevailing rains of forty days and forty nights, with expected disastrous flooding to follow, he was advised to quickly build an ark to house (and save) pairs of different animals. Noah, in an effort to care for these animals, laid fleece over the wooden floor of the vessel. During the long voyage, the animals were underfed, causing the sheep to shed more of their wool. At the journey's end, Noah found that the wool had matted together and had become, literally, a wall-to-wall carpet!

Think of the conditions inside the ark that might have brought about this change in the wool. It would have been warm in there, with sweat and uric acid dampening the wool. And imagine how the animals would have stomped the fibers under their hooves during their stay in the ark.

Felt was in use long before these tales were spread, but they shed some light as to how felt as a material was actually born. Historians believe that after the use of skins and furs as primitive body coverings, the human's first handmade material was felt. It remains a great survival aid to many who must cope with a harsh environment.

ABOUT NOMADIC FELT TENT-MAKING

The wall felts for circular nomadic tents, or yurts, are made while simultaneously rolling three pieces of different hardness (each one weighing about 44 lbs [20 kg]) (see page 123). Nomads use a camel or a horse to pull and roll these large felts—three layers of thick felts, including the weight of the water used to dampen them, plus the hides used to secure and close the bundle, are much too heavy to work by hand. Contemporary no mad felters have been known to pull felt bundles behind their bicycles.

A. Beating and separating the wool with sticks

B. Laying out wool for a felt tent wall

C. Blessing and rolling the bundle with the help of horses

D. A Mongolian "ger" felt tent

ARCHEOLOGICAL EVIDENCE

The British archeologist James Mellaart headed four excavations between 1961 and 1965 at the Çatal Hüyük mounds of the Anatolian plateau in Turkey. Çatal Hüyük, considered the world's first example of a true city, was a Neolithic settlement which grew into an interesting religious and major trade center. The excavation team unearthed a large wall painting (6 x 4.5 m) in an interior shrine. Within each of the five panels of the painting there were motifs of repetitive curvilinear forms resembling stylized antlered creatures. According to Mellaart's description, "Both patterns and edging technique are strongly reminiscent of felt appliqué." In 1963, tiny pressed animal fiber fragments found at the sixth level, considered felt remains, were identified by excavator

Ancient Çatal Hüyük wall painting, Turkey

botanist Hans Helbaek, of Denmark. Woven woolen and bast fabrics, however, were predominantly manufactured and already well known to these people around 6500 to 6300 BC.

In 1984 and 1986, several extremely important objects were excavated at an ancient desert tomb site, along the southeast edge of the Takuramakan Desert, in the western province of Chiemo, China. Among the items uncovered was a tall pointed black hat with stitched seams, a white seamed cap adorned with two short horn-like features of rolled felt fabric, and a white seamed felt sock. All of the items have been carbon-dated circa 1400 to 1200 BC and were known to be worn by peoples of Central Asia. This area, known as the Kingdom of Khoran, was a meeting place of different cultures from the East and West.

The exceedingly dry desert conditions were conducive to preserving the variety of objects of animal fiber, vegetable fiber, and metal, which were all found in excellent condition. Items like these have been depicted in various Chinese sculptures, reliefs, and paintings, but extant examples are extremely rare. This discovery marked the most recent finding and the oldest existing felt objects found in excellent condition.

THE NECESSITIES OF NOMADIC LIFE

The study of geographical regions around the world, especially Central Asia, where pure sheep breeds are still indigenous and plentiful, has allowed historians to piece together how the ancestors of contemporary nomads survived and flourished, and how they centered their lives around the uses of their animals' fibers and by-products. Their tent shelters were covered with thick protective handmade felt—the circular, domed roofs, walls, and ground coverings were all made of this wonderful felt. Their protective clothing had the strength and warmth of matted wool, in combination with skins and furs. Boots, hats, and large wrap coats protected the nomadic tribesmen from warring harms and dangers of severe climate. Auxiliary felted items such as bags, tent pole covers, saddles, blankets, talismans and ritualistic objects continue to help nomadic people survive to this day.

Stitched cap with horns, China

PAZYRYK COLLECTION

In southeastern Siberia, in the late 1920s, Russian teams directed by Sergie I. Rudenko led the discovery of the numerous objects in the Pazyryk collection of the Hermitage Museum in St. Petersburg. This vast Scythian attuned cultural revelation was unearthed in the great Ulagan Valley of the Altai Mountains in Kazakhstan; just west of where the borders of China, Mongolia, and Kazakhstan meet. It is one

Stitched boot liners, China

of the most renowned felt collections in the world, gathered from hundreds of burial chambers, including that of royalty. The objects have been radiocarbon-dated circa 430 B.C. and were extraordinarily well preserved in a tomb site that had flooded, then frozen into permafrost, resulting in an air-free state. The highly decorative and technically advanced objects of a variety of fine materials including gold, silver, leather, included woolen burial accompaniments produced from the fine undercoat wool of sheep. Horse saddles of leather and felt, which were sometimes dyed red or blue, were of extremely high quality. In adjacent chambers were items of everyday use, such as boot liners for men and women, caftans, bases for leather head decorations, black carpets, wall hangings, covers for bodies, and linings of sarcophagi. Still other finds include cushions, as well as women's hair accessories which were clumps of felted hair worn under and entwined in their real hair. Felt was also used for cut-out animal and birdlike shapes for motif decorations and was used in appliqué designs on bows, saddle covers, masks, covers for horses' manes, and more.

Among the most recognized works are four famous white swans, each about the size of an American football. As M.E. Burkett notes in her book, *The Art of the Felt Maker* (1979), it is possible they adorned the corners of a carriage for the dead and, like idols, they were considered to possess magical powers beyond that of simply spectacular decoration. These seamed felt birds were stuffed with plucked deer fur and

One of four Swans from the Pazyryk Tomb sites, Siberia

appliquéd. Another item that has come to be one of the most impressive felt objects in the world is the extremely large wall hanging (approximately 15' x 19' (4.5 x 6 m) which depicts in six repeat motifs a handsome, caped horseman facing a seated goddess holding a flowering branch. This work is renowned for incorporating appliqué, inlay, and embroidery techniques.

EUROPEAN EXPLORERS
During an expedition to western China by the British explorer Sir Aurel Stein, quilted shoes measuring 9¾" (25 cm) long were discovered. Whereas the tops of the shoes are embellished with a stitched motif of overlapping scales, the bottoms are knotted consistently over the surface of the sole. Dating from mid-eighth to ninth century B.C., this elegant work was found in a fort at

Appliquéd wall hanging (detail), Pazyryk Tomb sites, Hermitage Museum

the edge of a range of foothills known as Mazar-Tagh. Records of Tibetan, Chinese, and Khotanese settlements were found at the site.

In Noin Ula, Mongolia, at an altitude of some 4920' (1500 m) above sea level, another burial site containing preserved felt objects was found. In the burial chamber, multi-antlered, mythological creatures as well as birds were applied to the felt covering the floor and ceiling. Embroidery and other materials were also discovered. The larger work there has a central panel consisting of twenty-four spirals, along with a scene of animals in combat. At a site nearby were lacquerware bowls dating back to the year 1 A.D.

Idol dolls once belonging to a Barak shaman were acquired by the Danish explorer, Henning Haslund-Christensen, during an expedition to Urte-In Gol in the Chachar district of Inner Mongolia in the 1930s. The two felt dolls of cut and stitched construction rest inside a stitched, felt-lined bag. Other accounts have been written by Berthold Laufer (1930), Hans Bidder (1964), and others about felt idols symbolizing guardians or family members, which were placed in honorable positions in the yurt and given offerings of food even before the family members would partake themselves.

EAST ASIAN TREASURES
At the last stop of the silk road to the East, in the ancient capital of Nara, Japan, under the auspices of the Imperial Household Agency, is the

Polo Player Carpet, Shōsō-in Collection, Nara

Shōsō-in Collection of *denseihin*, meaning preserved above ground since their manufacture. These elite foreign gifts, sent to the Emperor, and fine quality domestic items made to be used in offering services, including instruments and costumes, date back prior to 752 A.D. Among these items are also imperial artifacts personally used by Emperor Shōmu and his wife, the Empress Kōmyō, which are made of silk, linen, leather, precious horn, felt, glass, and wood.

Although wool was considered a lesser material than silk for an Emperor, there is a distinguished felt carpet collection that includes the best existing examples in the world of eighth century A.D. works. Some of the most intricate floral detailing and color gradations found to date can be seen in the collection of thirty one kasen carpets, preserved in the north section of the Shōsō-in. Even the monochrome carpets (Shikisen) are of great interest, as it appears they may have been made larger in size and then cut in half. (Three of the four edges of one natural white carpet in particular appear to have been folded over during the felting process, whereas the remaining fourth edge has a keener, cut effect.)

Whether these carpets came from Korea or China, or lands beyond the Great Wall, cannot be clearly known. However, one of the carpets dedicated to the Great Buddha of Todaiji Temple by Empress Kōmyō at the time of the death of the Emperor, contains a Tempō-Shō-Hō eighth year (756 A.D.) seal, bearing the mark of the unified Silla Dynasty (668 to 918 A.D.) of Korea. This note is recorded in Kaneo Matsumoto's book, *Jodai-Gire, 7th and 8th Century Textiles in Japan from the Shōsō-in and Horyuji.*

In Japan's long history of textile arts, wool production and use is relatively recent. Yet a rare diary account of carpet making at a shrine in the city of Nagasaki, Kyushu, exists. During the Meiji Period (1804 to 1806), two Chinese were brought to Sui Shrine to introduce the techniques of carpet making. The color sketches drawn by a priest at the shrine gives a clear explanation of the tools and techniques employed by these foreigners. (See the illustrations on pages 8 to 9). Carpets were made in white, then dyed in large kettles with natural plant colors of blue, red, and yellow, and over-dyed to achieve greens and purples. It is also recorded that the carpet makers used a carding bow to carefully open the tufts of wool in preparation for felting.

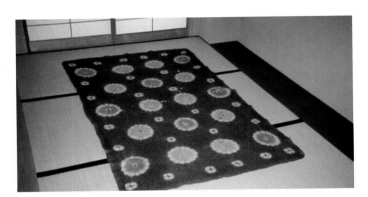

Natural tie-dyed felt Mōkosen carpet on tatami mat, Japan

Another special tie-dyed carpet, called Mōkosen and found in Japanese collections, is occasionally used today to cover the cool tatami mats in the room where guests assemble before tea ceremonies. Designs of brightly colored wheels or umbrella spokes help warm the atmosphere for special fall and winter tea ceremony festivities.

WOOL IN EUROPEAN AND SCANDINAVIAN HISTORY

Wool has long been a favored fiber in Europe and Scandinavia. In Italy, the wool guild Arte Della Lana was established in the 1400s. Quite possibly the oldest and still visible surviving illustration of felt being made is found on a wall in southern Italy. In ancient Pompeii, the city that was destroyed by the eruption of Mt. Vesuvius in 79 A.D., is a painted mural depicting a feltmaking shop belonging to a man named Verecundus; shown there are four shirtless men at work, kneading felt pieces over troughs on either side of a central hearth.

Verecundus' Workshop Fresco, Pompeii

As to written histories, the great epic poet Homer, living in the eighth century B.C., mentions felt in his tale of the *Iliad*. He describes Odysseus' leather helmet lining, among other items of protective battle dress, as being made of felt. Herodotus, the Greek historian of the fifth century B.C., described the use of felt by the Scythians. These two prime examples allow the interpretation that Greek interaction with nomadic peoples introduced feltmaking to the Greeks. Among Greek sailors, fishermen, and craftsmen, hats have always been very popular and various shapes of brims and functions were developed with felt as a prime material.

Carved design of felt hat of warrior women in Hercules' sarcophagus, 250–260 A.D., Konya, Turkey

Roman soldiers wore tightly fitted skull caps, felt boot liners, and thick felt armor vests, all so dense that they were able to resist both fire and the swipe of the sword. What's more,

Felted animal mask recovered from sunken ship, Denmark

Roman coins issued commemorating Caesar's assassination in 44 B.C. depicted a certain conical hat design which again appears on another coin minted during the reign of Antonius Pius in the second century A.D.

In Europe and the Nordic countries, many felt fragments have been found. In Norway, a bronze urn dated from 400 to 500 A.D. was found in a funeral pyre. Preserved inside the urn were two pieces of felt, which were wrapped around a dead man's leg. In the ancient town of Hedeby, Denmark (now part of northern Germany), an animal-shaped mask, possibly of a sheep or a bear, was pulled from between the boards of the hull of a sunken vessel. The ship, evidence of the Viking era (eighth to tenth century A.D.), was recovered in 1979. Tar, the weather-proofing for the hull, had saturated the mask and preserved it very well.

FELT IN THE MODERN AGE

Finns were said to beat the Russians because of their skiing expertise and hardy felt boots. The Germans during WWII approached a French hat-making factory in Chazelles-sur-Lyon to order felted socks made from Angora rabbit hair; if you consider this idea today it would be an extremely luxurious item. Since the medieval times, Magyar herdsmen slung "szür" cloaks over their wide shoulders, which were made from a coarsely woven wool yarn, and subsequently shrunken, or fulled. Gradually in the eighteenth and nineteenth century they became more decorative with hand embroidery and become known characteristically as Hungarian works of stunning cut-work appliqué by machine stitching. Other European clothes were fulled similarly in a shrinking process, subjecting the cloth to moisture, heat, and agitation. If the process was executed by foot, it was called waulking. Industrial blankets and military uniforms used fulled fabrics, often referred to as "boiled wool," because of its strength, drapability, warmth, and ease of production in large quantity. An important item for the well-dressed man was the famous top hat made from felted and brushed

rabbit hair. In England, The House of Christy, established more than 230 years ago, was the only company still known to produce the infamous bowler and formal top hat at the end of the twentieth century. Sadly, they went out of business in the 1990s.

Felt was still entirely handmade until 1830 when an American, J.E. Williams, patented the first mechanical process for manufacturing felt. Many operations still employ both hands and machines to produce the millions of yards of industrial fabrics, which one might find inside a piano, on the tip of a pen, or under the lapel of a man's suit.

Mother Nature has also been a splendid source for amazing felt works. There are native birds in Mongolia named Oranshovo (*Remiz-penduli-nus*), for instance, that select different qualities of wool and build themselves socklike nests with one opening. The construction is large enough for hatching two to three eggs. These nests are sturdy and provide shelter for the birds to return to year after year. The Mongols revere these constructions as sources

Oranshovo bird's nest, Mongolia

of power, beauty, and virginal purity, and say that because the nests only have one opening, when good things are gathered inside, they cannot escape. Mongolian friends tell me that these nests can be cut and used as children's boots, proof of both the material's strength and the bird's skills.

Another story, a bit dispiriting, relates to rock-hard fur balls found inside the second, undeveloped stomach of calves after they are taken to the slaughterhouse. These young animals are prized in Europe for their tender meat and are kept in stalls in dark barns. The fur balls, some the size of grapefruits, are the result of nervous licking, ingestion, and the constant pressure, moisture, pH acidic climate, and heat inside of the animal. Cats are commonly known to expel their fur balls, perhaps you've found evidence of this around the house or yard, but apparently at such a young stage, the calves have no ability to do so.

From Western Europe to Central Asia, although the advantages of felt products are known, they may be fading due to industrial interventions such a shepherd's yurt kit or the laminated rubber-ized raincoat. *Kepeneks* or herder's mantles, vests, yurt dwellings, carpets, bags, headwear, gloves, even teapot covers are still made by hand to comfort and serve. If we include the now numerous and ingenious ways that felt is being used for mechanical purposes—insulation, filtering, polishing, and so on—we can imagine a belt of felt running all the way around the world, even where sheep are not raised.

I have briefly discussed a few well-known felt finds, legends, and written histories here. Keep your eyes open and ask for assistance while visiting ethnographic museums around the world. I am sure you will be able to see many wonderful examples of the ultimate gift and uses of wool and of our best friend, the sheep.

Fur ball from calf, Holland

LOVE SONG
The boot called Touku
Makes a stamping sound;
A Torgut girl
Nods her head to me.

The black blaze camel
Stretches its nose ahead
The boot sewn in the Chalcha way
Blisters my feet.

The white blaze camel
Bends his knee
The boot sewn in an Olot way
Blisters my heel.

A thousand white sheep
Crossed the Mingat Pass;
My sweetheart's Touku
Is tied with a silken strap.

A song about the boots made by the Torgut women living in the district of Bulgan (southwest of Khowd) in the Altai mountains of western Mongolia. This love song is one of the nicest souvenirs I found during my first expedition to Western Mongolia in 1990.

Translation from Mongolian to English: Otto Farkas

In the many years of making felt and teaching feltmaking, I have come to realize a very important fact that must be understood well before anyone starts making felt. One must know the role the body plays in the process of felting and whether the tools and equipment, which are supposed to aid in felt production, are, in fact, causing any damage to the body. Paying attention to the work environment and body is important for a healthy and enjoyable feltmaking experience.

The worktable: Check the height of the worktable. When you roll wool, do not stoop too low or reach too high. Adjust the height of the table, if possible, or work on a different table if you feel any strain or discomfort. The worktable should be just below the height of your hips or at a comfortable height that when you roll, no strain is put on your lower back.

Posture pointers: Pay close attention to posture. Spread both feet as wide as the hips, and plant them firmly on the floor. You may also alternate one foot forward and the other back, then reverse positioning, to break up long periods of rigidity in the same position. During the rolling movement, do not lean over; instead, bend the torso over at the waist with feet and legs still in place. Use the weight of your upper body, applied through your lower arms, so only your arms move, not the entire body. Never overwork yourself and take breaks periodically. When you are working, ask yourself: Are both sides of my body being used equally? Is my breathing in rhythm with the physical motions? As a bonus, felting can help you get in shape, especially your arms, if you are positioning your body correctly.

Starting and ending your felting sessions with stretching exercises is also a good idea. Touch the ceiling with your fingertips; sway in place like seaweed in the waves; alternate running your hands down the side of one leg then the other to stretch at the waist, and so on. Hire a masseuse once a month or at times of tightness, or consider Yoga or Tai Chi. All of the abovementioned stretching, balance, and relaxation techniques will also help your felting technique.

Carpal Tunnel Syndrome, or chronic pain in the wrist area, now affects many people. This syndrome results from extended stress and overworking the fingers and hands, thereby affecting the many muscles connecting at the wrists. Felt artists are no exception. However, a lot of muscular distress can be eliminated if the whole of both arms, from fingertips to elbows, are kept straight during the rolling process. Also, make sure you add the weight of your upper body to provide pressure on the wool, instead of using only your arm muscles. Lean your upper body weight naturally into the bundle and allow your arm motion to rhythmically determine the back and forth motion. Turn your arms slightly inward so that the meatiest, muscular portion of the lower forearm is on top of the bundle and avoid rolling along the bone, which may cause painful bruising. You can also try using the weight of your legs and feet, while seated, to roll smaller, manageable, well tied-off bundles. This method also works your abdominal muscles, while giving your arms a breather!

Correct body position for rolling

Self-protection: When using greasy wool directly from a farm breeder, make sure that the wool is from a healthy sheep, and check for worms, insects, burrs, and vegetation. If foreign matter such as dirt or sand can't be simply removed by hand, remove it by washing (see pages 111 to 112).

The human skin is porous, and undesirable additives and unnatural color dyes continuously enter the body through our skin and fingernails. Therefore, be cautious about the substances you use that touch your skin, especially when working with children. It is important to select a soap that is gentle to the skin, especially if you are working with it all day. I always look for gentle, nonscented, colorless soaps and shampoos. Plant- and vegetable oil-based soap, such as olive oil soap, seem to be comparatively kind to the skin. Test the soap before use. No matter what soap you use, it may also be helpful to apply oil on your forearms, where the skin is tender, before starting a work session. Alternatively, cover your forearms with a pair of old cotton knee highs, cutting holes for your thumbs and hands to pass through. When using a bamboo mat or rough equipment, or even when using coarser wool for carpet making, for example, protecting the forearms from wear and penetration of the fibers is more comfortable.

Paying close attention to your body, the most important tool you have, is indispensable for the continued enjoyment of the magic of feltmaking.

Stereograph:
Sheep Shearing, US, 1890

ACID/ALKALINE
See pH/acid/alkaline.

BATT
A general term not limited to a specific fiber, these wide, carded, and layered sheets of fiber are convenient for large felt projects. Commonly known and used for cotton bedding or polyester quilt batting. The materials are prepared on large, wide drum carders or machine-needled into sheets.

BLENDING
Combining various fibers with wool or color mixing by carding. Similar to mixing paints in order to produce a new color or interesting surface quality to the work.

CARDING
The process of opening the clumps, or tufts of wool, separating the individual fibers, and aligning them in one direction by combing. One of several steps in the preparation process of spinning yarn.

COUNT
The fineness of the wool fiber corresponds to its rate of shrinking. In general, wool fiber is categorized as extra fine, fine, medium, or strong (coarse.) Wool trade is based on the fineness of the fiber in addition to the sheep breed. The fineness is expressed in two ways. (1) In the Southern Hemisphere, actual objective measurement of the diameter of the fiber (unit: micron Ì =0.001mm) is employed, and (2) in the Northern Hemisphere, the Bradford quality count is used. Under the quality-count system for worsted wool yarn, the larger the number, the finer the fiber. For example, 64s means that from one pound [0.45 kg] of scoured top wool, theoretically 64 skeins of 560 yards (512 m) each can be spun. The 64s wool is equivalent to 22 microns. For felting, 19.5 to 29.5 micron, or 56 to 70s, sheep wool is recommended. See chart on page 132.

CRIMP
Wavy, spiral, natural curling of wool fibers. The spirally curl is formed naturally by the dual structure of the fiber cells, not from applied pressure. Therefore, the natural crimp will not change over time and is virtually permanent. Generally, sheep with finer wool fibers have tighter curls or crimp. This characteristic enhances a wool's dye-affinity, its felting nature, resilience, and heat-retaining property, and makes a wool superior for spinning or felting.

CUTICLE/SCALE
The surface of the wool fiber is covered with scalelike cuticles jutting out toward the tip end. This projection of overlapping forms helps wool fibers entwine with each other, making spinning very easy, and is an important factor in felting. The unique chemical composition and delicate structure of the fiber gives wool the characteristic of repelling liquid while absorbing humidity, high fire-resistance capabilities, audio absorption, providing warmth even when wet, and more.

FELTING CAPABILITY
Felting capability is the visible percentage of shrinkage, when wool fibers, under correct conditions, migrate and entwine with each other. Making samples of various wool types offers the feltmaker an understanding of the shrinking speed, and the different types of surfaces possible for a finished project. NOTE: The speed of shrinkage is not the most important factor in felting; rather, it is knowing the shrinkage speed and other characteristics of a certain type of wool. One must select appropriate material(s) and use appropriate methods for that particular choice, to make a successful project.

FLEECE SOLD BY WEIGHT
This type of fleece comes from the winter coat shorn from the animal. It does not fall apart while being held because the staples, or clumps of fibers, have slightly entwined during growth. In the case of lamb's wool, or that of a short hair breed, the fibers do not entangle with each other and will not stay in the fleece form after shearing.

FULLING/HARDENING PROCESS
The second stage of the felting process after prefelting, in which the fibers are completely entwined with each other. The highest percentage of shrinkage occurs at this stage, and transforms the wool into a sturdy cloth or form. The same process was essential in the making of the famous Spanish Basque beret (knit), the Austrian Tyrolean jacket (woven), and the classic Scandinavian boot (wool felt structure only.)

FUR FIBERS

Hair from rabbit, fox, deer, mink, and so on.

GUARD HAIR

See outercoat/guard hair.

GREASY WOOL

Wool in its natural unwashed, unscoured condition, with fatty lanolin oil still on the fiber.

HAIR FIBER

General term for animal fibers or animal hair. Hair from animals such as alpaca, camel, and angora are generally coarse, stiff, lack crimp, have limited scales on the surface of the fiber, and undeveloped epidermis. The fulling capability and dye-affinity of these fibers is quite inferior when compared to finer sheep wool.

HANDLING TEST

The procedure to check whether the individual layers of fibers have entwined, forming into one solid fabric. Judge the handle by sandwiching the fabric, under light pressure with the thumb and fingers, while shifting it back and forth and checking for movement in the central strata. If the fabric is still relatively soft, the layers feel disconnected, and the direction of the outer fibers still visibly detectable, then additional fulling and hardening is necessary.

HARDENING

See fulling/hardening.

KEMP

The white or light grey, rigid, hair-like fibers that grow sparsely in the wool. It is coarse and comparatively short. It grows for a while and then gradually stops growing, eventually self-shedding. Kemp lacks crimp, resilience, a fulling nature, dye-affinity, and tends to be weak. However, it plays an important role before the sheep is sheared: It prevents the wool on the sheep's back from felting or compressing by creating passages for air circulation through the individual hairs.

NATURAL COLOR WOOL

Unlike chemical- or vegetable-dyed wool, this is the true natural color of the animal. There are varieties of browns, grays, and near blacks. However, these natural colors are being lost gradually to domestication and crossbreeding. Moreover, to facilitate factory processes and overcome dying problems, sheep with purer white undercoats, less the kemp and less the outercoats, are being bred.

NEEDLE FELTING

Rapid penetrating movements of barbed needles on a machine or executed by hand, in which the fibers are stabilized, entangled, and needled in place. This process is done when the fibers are dry, and is not usually done with 100 percent felting wool, but more commonly a nonfelting fiber, such as polyester or wiry wools which otherwise will not compact well. Combinations of different materials and design patterns are possible by needling fabric, yarn, or other mixed materials into the surface of a batt of fibers or finished fabric. Numerous visible pinholes are characteristic of needle felt.

NOIL

Nep (tiny woolen balls) and short fibers, combined with plant and foreign matter that are removed as waste in the process of combing when making tops, the raw material for yarn. This waste can creatively be carded into felting wool for interesting base effects.

OUTERCOAT/GUARD HAIR

Relatively thick, long, and coarse sheep wool that performs like a raincoat. This wool allows rain and snow to slide easily off the surface to protect the finer undercoat, maintaining the animal's body temperature. These fibers have few crimps, indistinct scales, and medullated shafts with a hollow center section.

FIBER COUNT AND USAGE CHART

Bradford Quality Count
(theoretical spinning capacity of wool)

Filament diameter (micron)

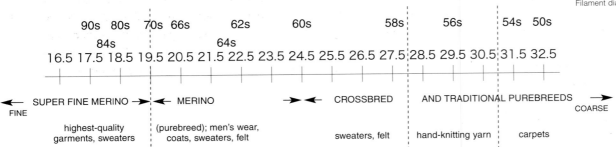

pH/ACID/ALKALINE SCALE

A number expressing the hydrogen ion concentration of a solution indicating whether it is either acid (i.e. vinegar, citric juices) or alkaline (i.e. milk of magnesia, mild soapy water), on a scale from 0-14. In relation to felting, the surface cuticles of the wool fiber have the characteristic reflex of opening outward when exposed either to strong acid or alkaline baths. The concept of the process of feltmaking utilizes this property to further force swollen fibers to entangle during the hardening phase. In factories, strong acids are used in lieu of soap for wet felting processes, however, when felting by hand, use soap or shampoo that is alkaline but when diluted has a strong influence on the wool but not your skin. A person with skin sensitivity should consider wearing rubber gloves and finding a soap, such as 100 percent olive soap, which is gentle to the skin while replenishing oils lost while working. Wool has a pH value of 4.9, and water is considered neutral at pH 7. Strong acid from pH 0 to 4; strong alkaline from pH 8 to 14.

PINCH-TEST

The procedure done to check whether the prefelt stage is reached. Deeply pinch several areas of a prefelted fabric or object with your thumb and forefinger, pulling up to confirm whether the fibers still appear separate or wholly entwined as a sheet of fabric or skin.

PREFELT; PREFELTED

Refers to the first stage of the felting process in which the fibers are entwined by adding slight agitation, i.e. rubbing by hand, or light rolling. This is a state between the fluffy dry fibers and the finished hardened product. This refers not only to a prefelt fabric, which is still soft and supple, but also to the state of a slightly formed three-dimensional object when the resist form is removed. Prefelt fabric is often used in the traditional technique of design-making: The dry prefelts are cut and embed simultaneously in the base layer fibers during the preliminary felting stage, and referred to later as "inlay."

ROLLING

One method of agitation during the initial fulling process. Felt fabric is wound around a pipe, dowel, or swimming pool noodle and rolled while applying pressure. Large projects are rolled on the floor; smaller projects are rolled on the worktable using the whole forearm from fingertips to elbows. For larger works, ropes are used and rolled between two to four people or drawn by a horse or camel, as in Mongolia.

SCALES

See cuticle/scales.

SCOURING WOOL

To prepare wool for carding by washing away the grease, oil, feces, dirt, and sand using a detergent.

SLIVER (also known as roving)

Carded and aligned wool fibers in a soft, untwisted, ropelike form in preparation for spinning. Also practical for felters.

TOPS

Separated longer fibers from washed, carded wool, made parallel by additional combing, that are aligned to form a ropelike sliver ready for the spinning stage of worsted yarn and felting.

UNDERCOAT/WOOL

Fine and soft sheep wool which plays the role of insulation that helps regulate body temperature on the skin surface. Because of its well-defined and uniform crimp, it takes in air very easily and has heat- and moisture-retaining properties. Also sometimes referred to as the "down" of the sheep.

WEB

The fibers are carded in narrow widths and entwined like a cobweb. It is the stage in the process before making a sliver.

WOOL

Raw, greasy protein fibers gathered from sheep. There are too many breeds of sheep to list here but some include Merino, Corriedale, Down type, New Zealand Crossbred, Romney, Navajo Churro, as well as numerous crossbreeds. Even within a single breed of sheep, the fibers may be distinguished between undercoat, outercoat (guard hair), and kemp. Breeds differ in fineness and coarseness of fiber, as well as length, curl and color, and are raised for a variety of purposes. Wool is made of Keratin and protein cells of complex amino acids. As for its structure, wool has an epidermis (cuticle) and has a dual-characteristic cortex causing it to spiral into its crimp; hair and kemp are medullated which means there are columns of space in the center cores of the fibers. The unique chemical make-up and intricate structure of the fiber gives wool the characteristic of repelling liquid while absorbing moisture, which means it provides warmth even when wet, as well as demonstrates high fire resistance among other outstanding qualities.

There is a variety of sheep breeds and different ways of preparing wool before utilizing it. Greasy wool should be washed, dried, and hand carded into mini-batts for ease in felting. White wool, combed into rope-like top, can be colored with vegetable or chemical dyes, however, starting off with purchased dyed wool makes for a convenient start. A variety of good felting wool is now readily available for those of us who don't have their own flock!

HALCYON YARN
www.halcyonyarn.com
800-341-0282
outside USA & Canada (+1) 207-442-7909
slu@halcyonyarn.net
12 School Street, Bath, ME 04530 USA
*One-stop shopping for a variety
of wool, novelty fibers, and equipment*

WILD TURKEY FELT WOOLWORKS
www.wildturkeyfeltmakers.com
6042 Franklin Road
Moravia, NY 13118 USA
(+1) 315-496-2308
Fine Merino top

THE WOOL SHED
Woolshed@juno.com
312 Oak Plaza Cove
Georgetown, TX 78628 USA
800-276-5015
Fine Merino and blends

Miriam Carter
603-563-8046
mcarter@cheshire.net
43 Charcoal Road, Dublin, NH 03444 USA
*Fine Australian merino wool in batts
with 22 colors available*

FILZRAUSCH
www.filzrausch.de
(+49) (0)551-67515
Fax: (+49) (0)551-5042508
info@filzrausch.de
Hagenweg 2/b, 37081 Göttingen, Germany

R.H. LINDSAY CO.
www.rhlindsaywool.com
617-288-1155
wool@rhlindsaywool.com
P.O. Box 218, Boston, MA 02124 USA
*Standard natural color wool tops and
scoured wool*

SEEHAWER UND SIEBERT
www.naturfasern.com
(+49) (0)7472- 3019
Fax: (+49) (0)7472-24207
info@naturfasern.com
Heuberger Hof 1, 72108
Rottenburg a. N, Germany

WOLLKNOLL
www.wollknoll.de
(+49) (0) 7977-910293
Fax: (+49) (0)7977-910488
Fritz@Wollknoll.de
Forsthausstrasse 7, 74420
Oberrot-Neuhausen, Germany

KARTEHUSET
www.kartehuset.dk
(+45) (0)65 99 19 19
Fax: (+45) (0)65 99 19 81
info@kartehuset.com
Vesterskovvej 8, DK-5792
Årslev, Denmark

ÅDDEBO ULL
www.addeboull.com
(+46) (0)294-10171
Info@addeboull.com
Nektarvägen 31, 81065
Skärplinge, Sweden

PIIKU
www.piiku.fi
(+358) (0)14-854 112
piiku@piiku.fi
Piesalantilantie 17, Fin-41900
Petäjävesi, Finland

PRO CHEMICAL & DYE
www.prochemical.com
800-228-9393
pro-chemical@att.net
P.O. Box 14, Somerset, MA 02726 USA

SUSAN'S FIBER SHOP
www.susansfibershop.com
920-623-4237
Fax: (+1) 920-623-0120
Orders only: 1-888-603-4237
susanfiber@internetwis.com
N250 Highway A
Columbus, WI 53925 USA

THE FIBER STUDIO
www.fiberstudio.com
603-428-7830
9 Foster Hill Road
P.O. Box 637
Henniker, NH 03242-0637 USA

WINGHAM WOOL WORK
www.winghamwoolwork.co.uk
+44 (0)1226 742926
Fax: +44 (0)1266 741166
wingham@clara.net
Freepost, 70 Main St.
Wentworth, Rotherham
South Yorkshire S62 7BR UK

Austin, Bridget
The Feltmaker's Handbook
Books Unlimited, Auckland, New Zealand
1988

Bawden, Juliet
*The Hat Book, Creating Hats
for Every Occasion*
Lark Books, Asheville, N.C., USA
1993

Belgrave, Anne
How to Make FELT
Search Press, Ltd., Kent, England, U.K.
1995

Burkett, Mary E.
The Art of the Felt Maker
Titus Wilson & Son Ltd., Kendal,
England, U.K.
1979

Damgaard, Annette
FILT – Kunst, Teknik, Historie
Forlaget Hovedland, Denmark
1994

Evers, Inge
Felt-making, Techniques and Projects
Lark Books, Asheville, N.C., USA
1987

Fergg, Monika and Jürgen
*Filz and Dorm – Spielerisches Gestalten mit
Fläche, Ball und Schnur*
Verlag Paul Haupt, Bern Switzerland
1999

Gordan, Beverly
*FELTMAKING, Traditions, Techniques,
and Contemporary Explorations*
Watson-Guptill Publications,
New York, NY, USA
1980

Hagen, Chad Alice
*Fabulous Felt Hats
Dazzling Designs from Handmade Felt*
Lark Books, Sterling Publishing Co., Inc.
New York
2005

Jacobsen Hvistendahl, May
Håndlaget Filt
J.W. Cappelens Forlag A.S., Norway
2000

Jacobsen Hvistendahl, May
Nuno Filt – Toving med ull og silke
N.W. Damm & SØn A.S., Norway
2004

Krag Hansen, Birgitte
Filt i Form
HØst & SØn, Copenhagen, Denmark
1992

Krag Hansen, Birgitte
New Felt Using the Felting Needle
Forlaget Klematis A/S, Denmark
2004

Lang, Marlène
Filz Kunst – Tradition und Experiment
Verlag Paul Haupt, Bern, Switzerland
2001

Nagy, Mari & Vidàk Istvàn
Filzen Mit Kinder
Wider Print, Debrezen-Jòzsa, Hungary
2000

Nielsen, Lene
Mosekonens filtebog
Skarv's husflidsbøger, Holte, Denmark
1986

Office of the Shōshō-in
Shōsō-in Exhibition Catalogues
Shōsō-in Office, Nara, Japan
1987.90.91.92.95.97.98.99.2001.02.04.05

Rex, Susan
*Dyeing Wool and Other Protein Fibers,
An Introduction to Acid Dyes*
Published by Susan Rex
2004

Ryder, M.L.
Sheep & Man
Gerald Duckworth & Co. Ltd.,
London, UK
1983

Ryder, M. L.; Stephenson, S.K.
Wool Growth
Academic Press, London, England
1968

Schmidt, Trautelore
Seidenfilz, herstellen und gestalten
Frech-verlag, Stuttgart, Germany
1992

Sjöberg, Gunilla Pateau
FELT – New Directions for an Ancient Craft
Interweave Press, Loveland, Colorado, USA
1996

Smith, Sheila; Walker, Freda
Feltmaking, The Whys and Wherefores
Dalefelt Publications, N. Yorkshire,
England, U.K
1995

Smådahl, Kristen Julie
Filting av Ull
Landbruksforlaget A/S, Norway
1989

Spark, Patricia
Fundamentals of Feltmaking
Fine Fibers Press, Salem, OR USA
1989

Spark, Patricia
Scandinavian-Style Feltmaking
Fine Fibers Press, Salem, OR USA
1992

Tourtillot, Suzanne J.E.
*Making Beautiful Beads: Metal, Glass, Fiber,
Polymer clay*
Lark Books, Sterling Publishing Co., Inc.
New York
2002

Traub, Monika
*Werkstoff Fliz-Grundlagen,
Kleidung und Accessories*
Monika Traub Verlag, Germany
2004

Turnau, Irena
*Hand Felting in Europe and Asia,
from the Middle Ages to the 20th Century*
Instytut Archeologii I Etnologii,
Warszawa, Poland
1997

Vickrey, Anne Einset
The Art of Feltmaking
Waltson-Guptill Publications
New York
1997

ABOUT THE AUTHOR

Raised in Boston, in the home of a wool and fiber merchant, Jorie Johnson studied textile design at Rhode Island School of Design. She opened her design studio, Joi Rae Textiles, in South Boston on the same Summer Street that was home to many of New England's fiber brokerage firms. She also studied textile design in Finland, where she was first introduced to Scandinavian felt boot-making techniques in 1977. Studying, teaching, and exhibiting in Finland was the start of her world travels seeking information about modern and ancient feltmaking techniques.

Jorie was among the artists exhibiting at the Fine Arts Museum of San Francisco's Artwear: Fashion & Anti-Fashion show (including the accompanying publication by Thames & Hudson, 2005). She has an affiliation with Julie Artisans Gallery in New York City and has art work in the collection of the Textile and Costume Department of the Victoria & Albert Museum in London. She has led workshops in private studios and been invited to teach at many international felt conferences, including those in the US, Japan, Hungary, Finland, Norway, Sweden, Denmark, Holland, the Republics of Georgia, Mongolia, and Kazakhstan.

Her work has been published in *Fiberarts Magazine*, *Surface Design Magazine*, *Shuttle, Spindle & Dyepot*, *Echoes* (UK), and several other European and Asian publications. Since arriving in Japan 17 years ago she has reopened Joi Rae Textile's Studio, which produces hand-felted body wear, accessories, hats, and items for interiors. In Japan she is a visiting university lecturer and international ambassador of sheep, wool, and felt. Currently she finds herself "Tra feltro e feltro." (Loosely translated as "all wrapped up in felt.")

The book was first published in Japan in 1999 and has been updated by the author for this long-awaited English edition.